THE TOTAL GUIDE TO COLLEGE LIFE

What Students Say:

This is the most complete college book I've ever read . . .

I found your book to be informative, accurate, and greatly helpful in dealing with college life. I enjoyed reading it and will do so again. Many of the ideas I found in your book have already been incorporated into my college living, and I am working on more. It is a wonderful book packed full of helpful hints to help the college student survive!

The book covers areas in my life in which I struggle.

The part I personally got the most enjoyment from was the section on Pranks. I consider myself to be an expert prankster, but I'll give credit where credit is due: yours were very good. I even used one of your pranks on one of my quadmates . . .

Your humor helped alleviate a lot of the pressure and unnecessary worry of unavoidable college conflict.

If I would have known half of what you talk about in your book as a freshman, I would have been far better prepared to tackle the college scene.

I thoroughly enjoyed your information concerning the 25 least-liked foods in the U.S. Armed Forces.

Your idea about studying a couple nights before, relaxing the night before, and getting up early (the day of a test) was a revelation for me. I tried your approach as an experiment on my Later Hebrew History midterm and it worked wonders for my grade in the class—I got an A. I thank you from the bottom of my heart.

The humor makes it readable, and the advice is invaluable.

It's encouraging to see that there are people out there who care about my transition to college life.

Of all the books I've read this year this is it was the most practical and enjoyable.

If there was any present I would give a high school graduate it would be your book.

THE TOTAL GUIDE TO COLLEGE LIFE

ALICE SLAIKEU LAWHEAD
Stephen LAWHEAD

Harold Shaw Publishers
Wheaton, Illinois

To our many teachers and professors,
the good ones and the bad ones . . .
   (you know who you are)

Copyright © 1997 by Alice Slaikeu Lawhead and Stephen Lawhead

Originally published as *The Ultimate College Student Handbook* by Shaw Publishers,
© 1983, 1989. This edition is fully revised and updated.

ISBN 0-87788-848-5

Revisions and updated material by Betsy Rossen Elliot

Cover design by David LaPlaca

Interior design by Nathan Young

Library of Congress Cataloging in Publication Data

Lawhead, Alice.
      The total guide to college life / Alice and Steve Lawhead. — Rev. and updated.
         p.   cm.
      Rev. and updated ed. of: The ultimate college student handbook. ©1989.
      ISBN 0-87788-848-5
      1. College student orientation—United States—Handbooks, manuals, etc.
   I. Lawhead, Steve. II. Lawhead, Alice. Ultimate college student handbook.
   III. Title.
   LB2343.32.L37   1997
   378'.198—dc21   97-486
                                                                     CIP

03   02   01   00   99   98

10   9   8   7   6   5   4   3   2

PREFACE

We are not college administrators trying to defend school policy, teachers urging you to study or parents wanting their children to behave. We are two people who went to five colleges and universities between us; who lived on campus and off campus; who were single part of the time and married part of the time; who got good grades and bad grades; who did some things wrong and some things right; who have many fond memories and a few regrets.

Everything in this book is based on the following convictions:

1. Your goal in college is to graduate with good grades.

2. A college is a business and a student is a customer.

3. Knowledge is power; to know how colleges and universities operate is to promote success.

4. You should have fun while you are achieving your goal.

5. There is more than one way to skin a cat.

CONTENTS

Great Beginnings 1

FRESHMAN ORIENTATION

Straight Answers to the Questions Most Frequently Asked by Entering-College Freshmen

Q: I've never been away from home before. Will I get homesick?

A: There's a good chance you won't. Our government is currently readying enough serum to vaccinate every college freshman against the dreaded *domecilia* virus that causes homesickness. You may, however, contract any number of other things, including swine fever, tetanus typhoid, black plague or athlete's foot.

Q: What is a Dean and what does it do?

A: Every college has at least one person named "Dean" whom everyone is allowed to call by his first name. It is his job to make sure the students maintain the high academic standards of the school—that is, to talk quietly in the halls, spit out their gum and keep their desks in straight rows.

Q: What is it like living in a dorm?

A: It is like living with a band of Hungarian gypsies in a telephone booth. It is like trying to maintain a meaningful relationship with a troop of hostile baboons. It is like having 137 mothers. It is like being trapped in a root cellar with Gomer Pyle. It is like spending the night with the Waltons—every night.

Q: What is the secret to staying interested in college?

A: Girls/guys. Any upperclassman can tell you girls/guys make everything more interesting (depending, of course, upon which sex *you* are).

Q: What's the best way to study for exams?

A: One of the easiest and most popular ways to study is a relatively new theory called I.A.O.—Information Absorption by Osmosis. The idea is that since the close proximity of books is beneficial, prolonged exposure to the written word is desirable. A tour through any college library provides ample demonstration of this method; you'll see hardworking students facedown in their books, busily absorbing away.

Q: What is there in the way of entertainment at college?

A: Late night studying for a test, lack of spending money, grouchy roommates and parents who constantly worry what you're up to. These are just a few of the things that stand in the way of entertainment at college.

Q: Can I waive classes which do not apply to me or are repetitive?

A: Yes, you can. This is sometimes very tricky. Most students simply prefer to wave to professors, friends, or casual acquaintances.

Q: What's a good way to choose a college?

A: Get together with twenty or more friends. Form a circle and everyone pick a number. The number closest to 27 starts by shouting out, "I'll take Vassar!" Continue until everyone has picked a college. Anyone who can't think of a college loses his turn and must take whatever's left over.

Q: I was president of my senior class in high school. Could I become president in college?

A: It isn't likely. In view of the tremendous expenditure of time and money involved in the promotion of a presidential campaign, most college students just can't hack it. And although many past presidents were college graduates, the American public has never yet voted a student into the White House.

Q: Many students get married in college. Is it easy to find a husband?

A: Yes. There are many husbands in college, but most girls would prefer to marry a single man instead. That narrows the field considerably.

Education: What's left over after you've forgotten the facts.

Memphis *Transit News*

Q: Is the food at college as bad as they say it is?

A: Of course not. It's worse. At most colleges the food is so bad students are required to sign a written affidavit swearing never to reveal the true nature of the food they eat. All students have to sign if they wish to eat and/or graduate. (Ask the head honcho of the cafeteria how much he or she pays in malpractice insurance.)

Q: What is this new pass/fail grading system colleges have now?

A: There is really nothing new about this system, which was popular during the Dark Ages. Classrooms then were presided over by tyrannical headmasters who ran around yelling at the students, "Either pass this class, or you fail!" Nothing has changed.

Q: What is the difference between GREs and SATs?

A: GRE refers to tests you take if you want to go on to graduate school after college; SAT refers to traffic on the Santa Ana Freeway, or those great big jets that go real fast and make a lot of noise—I forget which.

Q: What are my chances of getting through college without borrowing money?

A: 68,000:1.

Q: What does it mean when a course has a lab?

A: It means you'll only be getting three hours of credit for an eighteen-hour class.

Q: I've seen many bald men graduate from college. This leads me to wonder—if I graduate from college, will I lose my hair?

A: Findings from current studies are inconclusive. In one experiment, eight rhesus monkeys were enrolled at Yale University, and four others took jobs at a factory in Trenton, New Jersey. Of the eight Yale monkeys, only three graduated. Of the three, two were bald and the other remained normal (although it did change its hair color as a sophomore). Of the working monkeys, one was laid off and two others were promoted to plant foreman. The monkey remaining on the assembly line developed severe baldness; the rest showed no signs of losing their hair. Thus, scientists concluded that college *did* affect hair loss. However, the findings were later invalidated when it was discovered that one of the monkeys who was promoted was wearing a toupee.

TA5KS

According to Frederick W. Coons* you will perform five tasks during your years in college.

At times you may be aware of what you are doing; at other times you will be totally oblivious to what is going on. You will perform these tasks because you cannot do otherwise, because of the inevitable physical, emotional, psychological and spiritual dynamics of growing up, and because you have chosen to spend this period of your life in a learning situation.

1. *You will resolve your relationship with your parents.*

On one hand you may find yourself resenting their continued protectiveness; they demand a weekly letter, and in absence of that they'll call you up and expect a rundown on your latest activities. On the other hand you

will look to them for help in financing an important purchase or in talking to the dean so you can get taken off academic probation. You will be presented with the opportunity to "disobey" their wishes, but you won't want them to know about it. Basically you will wish for the kind of relationship with them that you are enjoying with your professors; you will want to deal with them as one adult to another. Depending on their willingness to "let go" (it will be harder for them if you are the youngest child or the only child) and your own degree of tact, this can be a messy, unpleasant experience or it can be a rewarding time where you come away with greater respect for them and they learn greater confidence in their child. But at any rate, by the time you graduate from college or leave college, you will to a great extent have made peace with your parents and established the ground rules for your continued adult relationship.

2. You will forge your sexual identity.

Up to this point, believe it or not, your mother and father were your primary role models for sexual behavior and sexual relationships. On the basis of new information that you get in college, you will come to either basically approve or disapprove of the relationship you observed as an example of how your adult sexual relationships will be handled.

If you haven't done so yet, you will probably wonder about homosexuality. If you didn't date much in high school, if you don't have a good track record of successful relationships with the opposite sex, you may wonder if you are truly heterosexual. As you listen to the exploits of the guys in the frat house or the confessions of the girls who share your suite, you will find that they are relating experiences far beyond your own. There is a danger in 1) believing more than 14 percent of what they say and 2) comparing your own experiences and activities to theirs unfavorably, assuming that they represent the norm or what is average, and you deviate from that to a greater or lesser degree.

And if that weren't enough, you will be confronted, overtly, with ideas about sex which are very different than what you have believed up to this point. If you go to a large state university,

there will be students who are living together off campus and on; there will be gay and lesbian rights groups; there will be sexual libertarians who are seeking converts to a loose sexual philosophy. At a conservative, religious college you may encounter much stricter standards than you are accustomed to, causing you to have guilt about past experiences and questions about your present urges.

If you come to college unsure of your own sexual identity and standards, you may find yourself confused as to what is right and what is wrong, acceptable and unacceptable, normal and deviant. But by the time you leave college you will have formulated, to a great extent, your adult sexuality.

"No one is exempt from talking nonsense; the mistake is to do it solemnly."

Montaigne

---

3. You will construct your own value system.

Even if you were a rebellious high school student, you probably came to college working with your parents' system of values. You recognized that they did not have a corner on truth, but you respected them enough to live more or less in accordance with their standards. Now, more than ever before, you are confronted with philosophies, ideologies, theologies, ethical systems and moral codes which are foreign to you. You are exposed to communism as an alternative to capitalism, hedonism vs. puritanism, atheism in place of Christianity. Everything is now open to question. If you came to college unprepared to weigh the relative value of these positions rationally (without being personally threatened), you could be in big trouble; if you are susceptible to personal criticism from those you admire, you could have some battles on your hands.

In response to the unrelenting pressure of assimilating new ideas, some college students "buzz out"—they commit suicide or undergo such a dramatic personality change that they are hardly the same person. They have had the value system rug pulled out from under them, and are left with nothing to stand on, no point of reference from which to operate. As an alternative, many students embrace a ready-made set of values which is presented by radical political, social or religious groups. This is not a totally unacceptable way of dealing with the crisis, and after leaving college most of the students who become involved in such groups moderate their position to include values which they eventually gain on their own.

Parents are bound to be upset by this values shift, but it *is* part of growing up and it usually doesn't last forever.

"An idea isn't responsible for the people who believe in it."

Anonymous

4. ● *You will come to terms with your need for intimacy.*

In college you will have a great need for closeness and sharing— intimacy—with another person. Usually this person will be of your same sex. This need for personal intimacy is not the same as sexual intimacy. Many students, sadly, are confused on this point and adopt a sexually promiscuous or sexually deviant life-style in their misguided search for someone they can be close to. This search need not (and probably should not) lead to a romantic encounter or marriage or a homosexual panic. Rather, it is the intimacy which develops when personal feelings and needs are shared with another who can serve as an encourager and partner. Ideally it is the sort of happy relationship which continues beyond the college years, as when roommates keep in touch years after graduation.

5. You will plan for your life's work.

You are not picking a job description or title at this point. Rather, you are broadening your field of choice. This is why you are going to college—to increase the possibilities of life's work. The continual revelation that takes place as you discover certain classes to be more interesting than others can be frustrating and/or rewarding. College serves the seemingly contradictory purpose of preparing you for a specific branch of work after graduation and at the same time expanding your horizons to include ever more possibilities.

Again, this wrestling match with your personal interests and ambitions may cause your parents anxiety. As a junior with an undeclared major, they may wonder what in the world you are learning in college—if anything— and whether or not they should continue to fund this very expensive soul-search. You may have similar thoughts. Many times the answer is to leave for a brief period of time, the advantage being that when (and if) you do return to college you are doing so for reasons of your own and not simply because it is the path of least resistance. At any rate, you will leave college (under whatever

circumstances) with a much clearer picture of your future than when you enrolled.

These are the five tasks you face, and no one will perform them for you. That does not mean there is no help for you. There *is* help. It might come through a close and sensitive friend; it might come through a professor who assumes the role of mentor for you; it might be found in the fellowship of like-minded peers in an established group; it might be available through reading a book (like this one) that gives you insight and information or challenge and comfort.

There is danger awaiting you as you set forth on this quest: danger in that you can get ahold of bad information, fall in with a destructive group, establish hurtful patterns of thought and action. In short, you may emerge with problems that will take years to heal, if ever.

But there is also opportunity. You may find that person or group who truly helps and encourages you toward health and wholeness; you may remain open to truth, and unaffected by the distortions around you; you may create a solid foundation on which to build a good life. It's possible—*likely*—that you will emerge a better, more complete and happier person than when you went in.

Adolescent Psychiatry, Developmental and Clinical Studies. Vol. 1, S. C. Feinstein, P. L. Giovacchini and A. A. Miller, editors, New York: Basic Books, 1971.

Hail To Thee My ALMA MATTER

There are thousands of institutions of higher learning in this country, and you have chosen or will choose one of them to be your school. You will pay money and expend effort in the hope of becoming educated. On what basis will you make your decision?

The Options

1. College. Mostly, when someone talks about college, they are speaking of the four-year, accredited school where one can graduate with a Bachelor of Arts or Bachelor of Science degree. It may be state-run, private or church-sponsored. Depending upon its academic emphasis, it may be called a teacher's college or Bible college or liberal arts college. Liberal arts colleges have as their goal to provide an education which equips graduates with the ability to think logically, act rationally and make

independent judgments about new ideas.

2. University. When a school has several colleges and a graduate school program, it becomes a university. A large state university may have, for example, a College of Veterinary Medicine, Business College, Law School, College of Arts and Sciences, etc. Within colleges and universities there are those institutions that stress research and those that emphasize teaching. Mainly, this has to do with the kind of faculty the school tries to hire. If the faculty are involved in their own research and/

or writing ("publish or perish"), that's a research school. If the faculty are not particularly pressured to conduct research and write articles and books, but are hired on their ability to communicate and teach, that's a teaching school. Most colleges and universities are a little bit of both.

3. Junior college or community college. These schools usually offer a two-year program that provides specific training (computer programming or child development, for example) or academic preparation for further college work at a four-year school. Some are not accredited, and some community colleges concentrate so heavily on extension-type courses in such things as cake decorating, assertiveness training, wildlife photography and Zen Buddhism that they should not be seriously considered by persons who desire authentic academic credentials.

4. Vocational-technical institute. To receive training in auto mechanics, electronics, cosmetology or welding, or to get the Licensed Practical Nurse designation, you go to a vo-tech school. These provide intensive, practical training for specific jobs.

5. Bible institute. Bible institutes sprang up many years ago with the purpose of providing practical study in the Bible and theology for persons who needed it to serve on the mission field or in the pastorate, but who had neither time, money, nor inclination to pursue a seminary degree (vo-tech for ministers, sort of). Work at a Bible institute can be done in

anticipation of attending a four-year school, after attending college, or—for some career paths—instead of attending college.

What Is Accreditation?

It's an effort to provide an evaluation of a school's program based on certain objective standards. There are six regional associations that determine their schools' rating (New England, Middle States, Southern, North Central, Western or Northwest), and they do so on the basis of a school's faculty, physical plant and facilities, library, academic standards, graduate placement and financial stability. Many perfectly good schools—Harvard is one—do not seek or need accreditation (*Harvard,* for heaven's sake!).

But most do, and if you think you might go to one school for a year or two with the idea of transferring later on to another college, or if you are considering some sort of postgraduate work such as medical school or a Ph.D. in psychology, you will find yourself in big trouble if you do your undergraduate work at an unaccredited school. Your biggest danger is that the school you want to enter will not recognize the credits you earned at the unaccredited school and refuse to transfer them.

So check out the accreditation situation at the school you wish to attend in light of your future career goals, however vague those goals may be at present.

Making Sense of It All

Now you are probably more confused than when you started. You wonder how to make sense of it all—how to pick The Right School. There are several factors to take into consideration before you decide.

It would be hard to underestimate the influence that your parents can exert when it comes to choosing a school. Some clues that your decision has been made for you: your father starts whistling the Michigan fight song around the house and has begun shelling out to the "Go Blue" alumni booster club; your brother was president of the freshman, sophomore, junior and senior class at Springfield College; your mother leaves tear-stained brochures on your pillow advertising the school she never got to attend— Missiprissy Women's College.

Since you will probably be getting most of your financial support from your parents in one way or another, they will want to have a say in where you go. If after careful consideration you find yourself in total disagreement with them, you should try to present your case in a rational, well-researched way. If you can get them to at least visit some other schools with you, so that you can *both* broaden your horizons of what's available, that's a good way to approach it. You might compromise by agreeing to visit their choice if they'll visit yours.

Money is also a key consideration. The private, academically superior schools are the most expensive. On the other end of the financial continuum, local junior colleges or state universities that are located in your home town are very inexpensive since you pay resident tuition, live at home and do not have to travel to and from school in the spring and fall.

Before you assume that the school of your choice is out of your reach money-wise, though, remember that different schools have different scholarships and financial aid sources, and that the amount of financial aid you get is going to be based on your projected educational costs. So although there are probably colleges which are simply out of the question, there are many more which may be in your range once you look more closely at methods of financing tuition and room and board.

You must, alas, also take into account your past academic record—the degree of preparation you received in high school and your current academic ability. If you graduated number 435 in a class of 476 at a public high school, you are *not* going to get into Yale (sorry you had to hear it here). In some states—like the one where we attended high school—all state universities and colleges are obligated to accept for enrollment any student who has graduated from a high school in that state, regardless of that student's academic record. Note, the university is *not* required to keep these students in school if they continue to do poorly, but they do have one semester to prove themselves. If you did poorly in high school and have low ACT and/or SAT scores, this may be your only option.

On a more subjective scale, you may feel that your high school experience did not adequately prepare you for the college work you wish to do, even though your class standing is good. This is sometimes the case with kids who went to a rural school that had a program deficient in, say, science but who want to go on to study pre-med. Sometimes the answer is to do remedial work at a junior college before attending the chosen college. Furthermore, if you just feel that realistically you cannot do well at M.I.T. or that you would not get an intellectual challenge at Elm Tree College, that realization will help you rule out some schools and focus in on others.

Finally, vocational goals will help you decide. If you are absolutely certain that you want to do commercial design, there's no point in attending a vo-tech school which has no art department, or a university with no commercial design instruction. And if you want to be a dermatologist, time and money could be wasted while you attend a nonaccredited junior college just because it's close to home. Your guidance counselor or academic advisor can direct you to schools which will help you reach your vocational goals.

While a high degree of motivation on your part can make the best out of a mediocre or bad

situation, you would do well to educate yourself about the different types of education offered by different kinds of schools; to consider accreditation and how it will impact on your further education; to deal compassionately with your parents' dreams for you; to understand the many ways of financing a college education; to assess your abilities and interests in light of the education you will seek; to explore your own career goals and the schools that are best equipped to help you reach them.

LITTLEWIT COLLEGE CATALOG
Credibility Gap, North Carolina

OFFICIAL COURSE DESCRIPTIONS

10 Astronomy

A survey of the major celestial objects—planets, stars, 747s and big, floating space things; a study of their characteristics and behavior in the universe. Students will learn basic astronomy methods, such as how to distinguish a planet from a galaxy, the difference between an asteroid and a telescope, and how to make everyone think you've really seen a UFO. All students will write a term paper on the subject, "Alien Life in the Universe: Where Do They Come from? What Do They Want? And Why Do They Like Slim Whitman?"

—3 hrs. credit

388 Foundations of Abstract Algebra

Vector spaces, polynomials, topological composition, eigen-values, elementary number theory are discussed. Development of mathematical concepts are traced from early Egyptian number painting to the invention of zero in Ohio. Final test requires that students memorize all integers from 1 to 100, add columns and pronounce astronomically large numbers correctly (see Astronomy 110). Prerequisite: two years high school algebra or three years "Sesame Street."

—3 hrs. credit

311 Independent Study in Biochemistry

This course offers two practical options: 1) the theoretical study of a particular topic in biochemistry or 2) cleaning up the laboratory and looking after the white mice. Student initiative and progress are considered as basis for final credit. The approval of department head is required. (Mops and pails can be obtained from maintenance department; feeding schedules for the mice are posted near the cages.)

—credit: To be arranged.

418 Avian Biology (Urban)

Ornithological study of various species of common city birds. Class work related to field experience as students discover how to spot birds in large metropolitan areas. Techniques of identification and taxonomy explored. Topics covered: Pigeon Population in U. S. and Abroad (And Why There Are So Many); Puzzling Pigeon Facts; Pigeons as Pets.

—3 hrs. credit

257 Practicum in Piano Pedagogy

Focus on preparing student to give instruction on the piano. Students will listen to and evaluate performances by amateurish piano students, develop techniques for winding the metronome and watch films of people playing the piano incorrectly. Prerequisite: two major piano concertos, five hit songs or one Billy Joel concert.
—1 hr. credit

499c Organized Crime (workshop)

A short history of organized crime in the U. S. will be presented with emphasis on its relationship to contemporary institutions. Also, an examination of the influence of crime on the moral values of criminals. Students will be divided into small groups for workshop experience in racketeering, bootlegging, numbers running and bribing public officials. Each student will present to the class a summary report on a personal project. Pick one: bank robbery, extortion, tax evasion, kidnapping. There will be one field trip—six weeks n Joliet State Prison. Prerequisite: viewing *The Godfather* (parts I and II) and understanding Marlon Brando's speaking parts.
—5 hrs. credit

6 Philosophy—Knowledge and Reality

Systems of thought on the reality of knowledge and the reality of reality, as well as the more basic knowledge of knowledge are examined. Students are taught the fundamental practices of determining whether something is real and are encouraged to find out if they know anything. Readings in the works of major philosophers are inspected for resemblances to knowledge. The contributions of Plato, Oristhenes, Heidegger, Leno, and Rooney (Andy) are reviewed. Prerequisite: Abnormal Psychology 210.
—3 hrs. credit

111 Survey of Great American Poetry—Poe to McKuen

Great American poets studied. Analysis of the poem as posterized wall decoration and big moneymaker considered. Students will manufacture their own pseudo-poems after the manner of McKuen. (Negotiating a publishing and recording contract may be covered if time permits.) Jack Frost's great poem, "Stopping by the Woods on a Smoggy Evening," Carl Sandpile's homage to an eternal city, "Muncie;" Poe's classic, "The Trained Crow" and "Colorado" are critiqued.
—3 hrs. credit

323 Argumentation and Debate

Group discussion as an effective method of problem-solving. Attention moves progressively from the study of argumentation, analysis and discussion of issues, to name-calling, harassment, boycotting and brawling. Students asked to build repertoire of argumentation techniques, including: hurt, disgust, temper tantrums, nervous fits, pitiful crying and righteous indignation. Topics of interest form basis of reports by class members. Examples: "How to Win an Argument You Didn't Start"; "Kung-Fu as a Persuasive Technique"; "Kissing and Making Up"; "The Joy of Compromise." Required text: *How to Be Your Own Best Friend.*
—4 hrs. credit

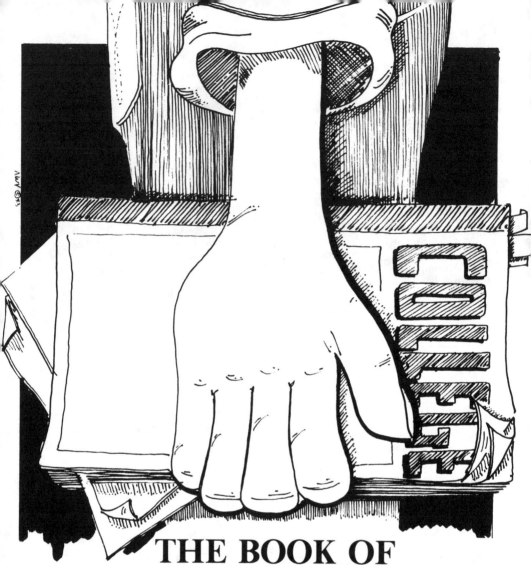

THE BOOK OF KNOWLEDGE

In his first day at camp a new Army recruit is given a rifle and told by his drill sergeant, "Men, this is a rifle! It is your friend! You will sleep with it; you will eat with it. You will keep your friend clean at all times! You will learn to care for your friend as you would care for yourself! Your friend will keep you alive!"

The same sort of thing happens in college, only they don't make such a big deal out of it. They give you a college catalog—along with a bale or two of other printed matter—and tell you to memorize it.

Most students sift through the stuff and eventually toss it away by the handfuls. The catalog is left to gather dust under the bed with forgotten dirty socks or it's used to prop up the short leg of the desk. But the catalog is not an ordinary piece of junk literature—the kind you'll see handed out by the thousands throughout your college career.

If you've got a question about some niggling detail of academia, no matter how obscure, the answer is bound to be in the catalog somewhere. That, very simply, is what it's for. In fact, the catalog is so important that many colleges and universities put it and other official publications on the World Wide Web.

And you might as well read it at the start because it's going to haunt your entire student lifetime. You're talking to the bursar for example; you want to know if you can pay half your tuition now and half in a couple weeks when your work-study check comes in. The bursar will look at you coldly. "No," she'll say. "Didn't you read the catalog?"

Or you go talk to a professor about taking an incomplete in Statistics. "Can't help you there, sport," he says. "You should have read the catalog."

Reading the catalog will save you from all sorts of desperate, eleventh-hour dramatics. Knowledge is power. If you *know* the catalog, when you find yourself begging for clemency from a reluctant petty official who begins quoting you chapter and verse, you can play and maybe beat him at his own game. At least you'll know where you stand.

The catalog is your friend. Read it. Study it. Refer to it often. Keep it clean. It's chock-full of all sorts of buried gems that you can dig out and use to your benefit.

One of the benefits is that since nobody else will have read the catalog, you'll be looked upon as something of a sage, a superbrain. Fellow-students will flock to you for advice; you'll be well-liked and popular. And who knows? You might even get a date or two out of it. Now you're learning what *real* power is!

"Like a good fundamentalist knows the Bible, a good student knows his catalog inside out. If it is not in the catalog, it does not exist."

from *Surviving the Undergraduate Jungle*

So you say you aren't popular on campus: your roommate won't introduce you to his mother, and your professors cross the street and walk on the other side when they see you coming? You say you're unhappy? Is that what's bugging your baby blues, bunky?

Well, cheer up! There's hope, even for you. Follow these simple instructions and you won't have to spend four years in solitary.

MS. MANNERS' RULES OF STUDENT ETIQUETTE

1 You may not have had to share a room with anyone since you were eight years old and your brother moved to the basement. This is a disadvantage when it comes to living successfully with your roommate. Respect his right to privacy; look at your personal mannerisms from his point of view and ask yourself every day if you are doing your very best to be fun to live with.

2 You may have been the class clown in junior high, but your career as a cutup has got to stop. This is the major leagues, and there's no place for the guy who organized the entire class to simultaneously drop their books in study hall or the girl who considers her professor's lectures a series of straight lines.

3 Maybe you *do* know all the answers, maybe you *do* find the professor and the class enormously stimulating to your vocal cords and maybe you simply *must* disagree with Mrs.

Strange's entire philosophy of education, but you *won't* make points with anyone by monopolizing class time with your wisdom. In large lecture classes your participation is almost formally discouraged and even in small seminar classes you must realize that there are others who need to share their thoughts and insights but will be unable to do so when you beat them to it all the time. Speak up only when called upon to do so, when you have a crucial contribution or when asking an important question.

"Better to remain silent and be thought a fool than to speak and remove all doubt."

Abraham Lincoln

---

4 When it is time for you to participate, make sure that you have listened to the comments from the instructor and students preceding yours. What

19

you have to say will be appreciated when it takes into consideration what has already been said. You're going to look like a fool (worse, a boring fool) if you spend five minutes explaining a theory—presenting it as some electrifying new insight—that was in yesterday's reading assignment or just addressed by the redhead in the back row. Refrain from digressions. Your tangent point may be interesting, but may also be resented if it wastes valuable class time.

"Manners must adorn knowledge and smooth its way through the world."

Lord Chesterfield

5 When you are called upon for an answer and you don't have it, either admit the fact and sit down or skillfully ask a question back again. Don't ramble or improvise; just get in and out quickly.

6 Professors dislike . . .
a. Class loudmouths.
b. Students who remain invisible throughout the semester and then materialize with a term paper that is two weeks late or a gripe about a poor grade.
c. Students who monopolize class, after-class and office time with unimportant matters; those who talk their ear off about trivial matters; those they have to avoid.
d. Students who try to buddy up to them and use a personal relationship to get a good grade.

Professors like . . .
a. Students who work up to their ability.
b. Students who communicate with them even when they aren't steamed about a bad grade.
c. Students who are willing to learn from their mistakes.
d. Students who improve their performance over the course of the semester.
e. Students who show up for

class and give eye contact while they are there.
f. Students who are friendly and respectful.
g. Students who complete assignments on time or have a *good* reason why not.

7 Try to find your niche on campus. Where do you belong? What are your responsibilities? Different things will be expected of the junior class president than a commuting part-time student. This has nothing to do with your worth as a person or your right to an education or your need for acceptance and affection from fellow-students and the faculty and staff. This means that you may have to come to understand that the entire university is not at your beck and call; or that you do have a right to protest an unfair grade; or that you have a legitimate right to ask your professor to account for how your grade was determined; or that the administration is not obliged to change its dress code just because you like to go barefoot in the winter. They don't call it the student *body* for nothing. While college life may provide you with the most freedom and respect for your individuality that you will ever have, it also has the responsibilities of community. Do your best to figure out what the body is like and then figure out what part *you* are.

8 If you choose to be the campus dissident, there will be a cost. Understand this. We all owe a great deal to the courageous individuals who, throughout history, have sacrificed their popularity for a cause. But they often did it at a personal loss. If you truly do march to a different drummer, seek out—through your church, club or social group—support for your actions. You may not be the most popular kid on campus, but you will need at least one close friend to help you through the stress and difficulty of being a square peg.

REVELATIONS

College is an eye-opening experience. You can help ease your culture shock the first days and weeks on campus by realizing that . . .

I. Your values are peculiar to you, alone.
II. You're not the seasoned veteran you thought you were.
III. Dorms are designed for maximum noise proliferation.
IV. One is a lonely number—even in a crowd.
V. True friends are sacred gifts from a loving God.
VI. The more studying you have to do, the more enticing the distractions.
VII. Everything you know is wrong.
VIII. People cannot be judged by their covers.
IX. College is not as difficult as you thought it would be, nor as exciting.
X. No one cooks like Mom.
XI. Your roommate belongs to a lower order of animal life.
XII. Everyone is smarter than you, and better prepared.

XIII. An honestly voiced opinion is an invitation to an argument.
XIV. You are six months behind all current events.
XV. You are not the open-minded humanitarian you believed yourself to be.
XVI. You cannot possibly read every book on the syllabus.
XVII. Standing in line is a way of life.
XVIII. Parties are boring.
XIX. There is never enough money.
XX. Your instructors don't lie awake at night wondering how to make their courses better, easier and more stimulating for you.
XXI. Your roommate does not lie awake at night wondering how to make life better, easier and more enjoyable for you.
XXII. There is not enough time to do everything you have to do.
XXIII. You have so much time on your hands you may die of boredom.
XXIV. Getting a date is every bit as impossible in college as it was in high school.
XXV. Temptation comes in many forms, all of them designed to prevent you from sleeping and/or studying.
XXVI. Many of life's problems cannot be solved by dropping a class.
XXVII. Many of life's problems *can* be solved by dropping a class.
XXVIII. The best-looking girls/guys are married.
XXIX. You are making your own decisions, and most of them are right.
XXX. Your high school letter sweater impresses no one.
XXXI. No one remembers your name.
XXXII. The day you skip class is the day they give a pop quiz.
XXXIII. Entertainment is expensive; fun is cheap.
XXXIV. You can actually learn from other people.
XXXV. There's no place like home.

Money Matters 2

YOUR RICH UNCLE

Elliott Rosewater, the simple-minded hero of Kurt Vonnegut's *God Bless You, Mr. Rosewater,* described the flow of money through the land as a river, a secret river—and, if you were very lucky, someone would take you to its riverbank, thrust a bucket into your hand, and show you how to fill your bucket from the money river.

They ought to hand out buckets when you get to college, because a money river would sure come in handy. (If your last name is Rockefeller, Pillsbury, Kennedy or Hunt, you can skip this article—your bucket is already in the river.)

In times past there were numerous money rivers students could go to for help. Lately, though, many of these sources have dried up in the economic drought. Others that ran sloshing over the banks have been reduced to a turgid trickle. It's a lot tougher to get money for college now than it was ten years ago.

Tough, but not impossible. You have to know where to look and how to use your bucket.

Can You Speak Mumbo-Jumbo?

Learning the lingo is the first step. Do you know your SEOG from your PLUS? Can you tell the difference between a Pell and a SAR? Do you know what CW-S, GSL, or FAFSA is?

No? Then you've come to the right place. In order to make sense of this alphabet soup you must understand the vocabulary of the U. S. Department of Education and other financial aid establishments. Here's a crash course in translating mumbo-jumbo into English:

SEOG	=	Supplemental Educational Opportunity Grant
SAR	=	Student Aid Report
CW-S	=	College Work-Study Program
PLUS	=	Parent Loans for Undergraduate Students
Pell	=	Pell Grant Program
FAFSA	=	Free Application for Student Aid
FFS	=	Family Financial Statement
PL	=	Perkins Loan
GSL	=	Guaranteed Student Loan

MINORITY STUDENTS

Booklets on financial aid for minorities in various fields are published by Garrett Park Press, Box 190, Garrett Park, MD 20896. Phone them at (301) 946-2553.

One of the most comprehensive listings is _The Directory of Financial Aid for Minorities,_ by Gail Ann Schlachter and R. David Weber. Available from Reference Service Press, 1100 Industrial Rd., Suite 9, San Carlos, CA 94070; phone (415) 594-0743.

Breaking the Code

Once you know the code, the next step is to become familiar with the programs, or aspects of the programs the initials describe. On we go . . .

Basically, all the initials refer to loan and grant programs of the federal government and the forms they use. A grant is free money; a loan, as you know, must be repaid—with interest. There are two different grants, four different loans, and one that is neither a grant nor a loan; you have to earn it yourself.

Here they are:

Pell Grant—As the name implies, this is money that doesn't have to be repaid to Uncle Sam.

Every year Dear Uncle places in qualifying schools enough cash to help out his needy nieces and nephews. The only catch is that you must demonstrate just how needy you are. The greater the need, the more cash the school will "give" you. Most schools don't actually _give_ you anything; they just deduct the bestowed amount from your tuition tab.

Supplemental Educational Opportunity Grant—Like the Pell, the SEOG is a cash gift to help defray expenses. Unlike the Pell, the SEOG works on the principle of "first come, first served." In other words, the Department of Education gives each school a set amount to make available to students. When the money is gone, that's it—no more SEOGs for the year. That's why you want to apply for this one as soon as possible. Each school sets its own deadlines, so check it out and be ready.

Stafford Student Loans—These are relatively low-interest loans guaranteed by the federal government. There are two kinds: subsidized (need-based) loans and unsubsidized (non-need-based) loans. These loans are awarded only as part of the aid packages put together by colleges. And like the rest of the aid package, you must file the FAFSA form.

Perkins Loan—This is a loan (what else?) that goes directly to the students whose surname is "Perkins" (har, har, just kidding, everybody). Its low interest rate of 5% makes it almost as good as free. Arranged and administrated by the school itself, one nice feature is that you don't have to start repaying it right away. You start six months after you leave school, whether you graduate or drop out. In some cases you can put off paying even longer by joining the military service or becoming a teacher in a depressed economic area, for example.

Guaranteed Student Loans—The major difference between this loan and the Perkins is that this one is made to you through a bank, credit union or savings and loan association. These loans are insured or "guaranteed" by the federal government. That means they'll cosign on the loan for you so that the bank will let you have the money even though you're only a poor student with no collateral and an uncertain future. See, Uncle Sam has faith in you; he believes that once you're educated, you'll find a wonderful job and the money will just pour in and you'll be able to repay the loan. The bank believes in Uncle Sam; they have grave doubts about you. (Actually, the government is starting to have its doubts, too, in view of the fact that the repayment of these loans has been poor in the past. Some people say the future of this whole program is in jeopardy because of the dishonesty of students who don't give the money back when the time comes.) But as long as Uncle guarantees it, the bank will let you have the money for low interest, payable beginning six months after you leave school. You get an application from the bank itself, not from the school, although the financial aid office must verify your legitimate educational expenses to the bank.

Parent Loan for Undergraduate Students—These are loans to the parents of undergraduate students (well, what did you think?) made by banks, credit unions or savings and loan associations. Comparatively speaking, they are not what you would call low interest. Graduate students can also get these loans, as well as independent undergraduates. The big feature here is that you don't have to prove financial need. But (and it's a big but) you or your parents must start repaying the money within sixty days of receiving it—in other words, while you're still in school. Ouch! However, in some situations repayment can be deferred to a later date (if the loan is in your name, for example, and you are still in school or have entered active military duty).

College Work-Study—Neither a grant nor a loan, it's a job. Basically, work-study is a program similar to the SEOG, except you earn your money instead of getting it outright. You apply, and if you qualify you are assigned to a job, usually somewhere on campus. The rest is up to you. Put in your hours, do your work, and you get a check. The good part is that, unlike a regular job, the financial aid office will take into account your class schedule, your academic progress, etc. and your work hours will be juggled around you, rather than vice versa. This *is* a type of federal financial aid, which means that there are forms to fill out, deadlines to meet and qualifications to be considered. There is also a ceiling on how much you are allowed to earn in any given term. Do not expect fast-tract high-level executive-type positions; expect the dregs—jobs that any boob can handle. At some colleges, *all* jobs are part of CW-S and to be a part of this program is the only way to work on campus.

"Don't marry for money; you can borrow it cheaper."

Scottish proverb

Red Tape and Paperwork

Of course, where the federal government is concerned there is always a mountain of red tape and paperwork to be done—forms to fill out, schedules to meet, deadlines to squeeze under, statements to prepare, letters to write, etc., etc., etc. Each of the above-mentioned programs has its own unique system of red tape and paperwork. The best way to prevail is to get in touch with the school you'll be attending early and learn firsthand what their requirements are—they vary slightly from school to school.

Next step is to request the needed forms. In some cases the same forms are used for different grants and loans. The reason for this is because you are allowed to sort of mix and match loans with grants and build the necessary financial aid package for yourself from various sources.

For example, you may qualify for a $600 Pell grant and a $400 per month work-study job. Tuition is $1800, and with living expenses you're shy $800; so you take out a GSL for that amount and you're all set. What you have done is build what a Wall Street broker might

call a financial aid portfolio which meets your needs, even though no single source would cover the entire tab.

And the key to this system? The SAR—Student Aid Report. This is the form that comes up with the little number that tells you how much money you qualify for (not necessarily how much you will receive. That's up to the school, the funds available, etc.). The SAR is based on another form, the FAFSA which is the Free Application for Student Aid form. The SAR takes the information from the FAFSA and determines your "need."

"If you think education is expensive, try ignorance."

Derek Bok
President, Harvard University

How Needy Are You?

Need is an interesting concept. Most simply, it is the difference between your cost of education and what you and/or your family can afford to pay. It really has little to do with actual money or what you *think* you can afford, because the costs of education vary so wildly.

For example, you may well be able to afford to attend the small state school in your home town—if you live at home and work part-time to pay the tuition of $500 per semester.

But suppose you want to go to school at the university sixty miles away where tuition is $1500 per semester and you'd have to live in the dorm. The more expensive school would therefore be out of your reach.

Hold it! Not necessarily. Generous old Uncle Sam is not concerned with practicalities at all. If you *want* to go to the more expensive school, so be it. He's behind your decision all the way. He'll help you pay for it.

The point is that even though you could pay your own way if you went to a cheaper school, your decision to go to a more expensive school created "need" where none existed before. So what if your dad could give you an all-expense paid education at the University of Texas—you want to go to Princeton! That creates need, need that can be reflected on a FAFSA form. The FAFSA takes all this consideration—your family's income, family size, tuition at the desired school, room and board, fees, book and supplies— everything that could have a bearing on the final tab of your education.

Then the sly geniuses who evaluate the FAFSA forms work their slide-rule magic on the information you provide them and voila! you get an SAR in the mail which tells you how poor you are. Poor, that is, in relation to the school you want to go to. Choose another school and you might be more or less impoverished, depending on what it costs to go there.

So don't let expense stand in the way of attending the school of your choice. Often the more needy you

are, the better off you are, from a financial aid point of view.

Tip of the Iceberg

That about covers the major points of the federal financial aid structure. But it barely scratches the tip of the financial aid iceberg, so to speak. Whole books have been written about financial aid and various places you can get help for education. There are thousands of private and institutional grants, loan and scholarship programs—little pockets of money all over the place just waiting for the right student to come along and find them. The best, and sometimes the only, way you can find them is to dig them out. Get ahold of some books on student aid, write for the pamphlets—in other words, dig, dig, dig.

Below are some good places to start digging.

One building—Your local public library is probably the best place to start. They normally have application forms on hand as well as copies of government publications you can have for the asking.

Two booklets—
1. *The Student Guide* from:
   The Federal Student Aid
      Programs
   P.O. Box 84
   Washington, D.C., 20044

This is the cursory guide to the programs discussed above. It'll tell you all you need to know to start your financial aid quest.

2. *Need a Lift?*
The American Legion
National Emblem Sales
P.O. Box 1050
Indianapolis, IN 46206

Not about hitchhiking, this is one of the most comprehensive guides to current financial aid around. It lists thousands of sources and references thousands more, complete with where to write for more information. You can also get a copy by checking at a local American Legion Hall.

A good book—See also *Don't Miss Out* by Anna Leider, Octameron Publications, Alexandria, VA (updated yearly—so far).

This book has been called the most comprehensive guide to getting money for education yet produced. It's well-organized, easy to read and covers the territory with a fine-toothed comb. Read this book, study it and refer to it often and you'll be light-years ahead of the next guy. Why, you'll probably know more than the financial aid officer at your college! Check it out at the library or better yet, buy yourself a copy. Any bookstore will be happy to order you one. It's worth its weight in scholarships.

SCHOLARSHIPS AVAILABLE!

We all know that 6'7", 285-pound linebackers can get a free ride at almost any school in the country. But if Mother Nature didn't bless you with such awe-inspiring vital statistics, you can still qualify for an all-expenses-paid four-year stay at the university of your choice.

"How?" you ask. Well, we predict that full scholarships are instantly available for the first student who . . .

. . . creates cold fusion with a Mr. Coffee and a jar of Tang.

. . . demonstrates a feasible means of trimming the cost of a Stealth Bomber from $20 billion each to 2 for $39.95 billion.

. . . documents the nutritional superiority of Hagen Däz Double Fudge over bran flakes.

. . . shows that the National Debt can only be erased by doubling the salaries of college and university administrators nationwide.

. . . provides the algebraic formulae necessary to prove that time = money, knowledge = power, and one oz. prevention = one lb. cure.

FINANCIAL AID THROUGH THE MILITARY

With the advent of the volunteer Army (and Navy and Air Force), your generous Uncle Sam is trying to make it very attractive for you to seek your future in the armed forces. One of his strategies is to help finance your college education in exchange for a stint in the service. There are several options:

1. *Military academies*—There are five in all, providing training for the Army, Navy, Air Force, Merchant-Marines, and Coast Guard. If you get into one of the academies all expenses are paid. Of course, there's the obligatory letter from your Congressman or Senator in order to be accepted, and the physical and academic requirements are pretty stiff. But if you're looking for a prestigious placement, you might want to go for it.

2. *R.O.T.C. (Army)*—In exchange for tuition, textbooks, lab fees and a tax-free subsistence allowance while you are in school, you agree after graduation to attend six weeks of training with the Army after which time you will receive a commission as a second lieutenant. Then you will be encouraged (yea, verily, *required*) to accept a regular army commission and serve actively for four years. R.O.T.C. = Reserve Officer's Training Corps.

3. *A.F.R.O.T.C. (You guessed it—Air Force Reserve Officer's Training Corps)*—You will be reimbursed for tuition, room and board, and given a monthly stipend to cover expenses if, after graduation, you will accept an Air Force commission and serve actively for four years (five if you

have flight training).

4. *N.R.O.T.C. (Navy and Marine)*—Like the Air Force, the Navy will pay tuition and room and board, and throws in books and fees along with a monthly stipend for expenses. After graduation, you accept a Navy or Marine commission for four years active duty.

5. *Veterans' benefits*—Of course, if you've already served your country you know that you are entitled to certain financial-aid-type benefits which we won't go into here. What you may *not* know is that if you are the child of a veteran, especially one who was killed or totally disabled while in the service, you may also be eligible for some real help in financing your education. The American Legion and its various auxiliaries and chapters offer scores of special scholarships and loans to relatives of servicemen and women, like the Marianas Naval Officers' Wives' Club Scholarship or the General Clifton B. Cates Memorial Fourth Marine Division Association Scholarship Fund. If you are interested, check it out. Contact the local Veteran's Administration office near you and get more information. Also, read *Need A Lift?* (see "Your Rich Uncle," p. 26)

School Sponsored Scholarships

DON'T erase

E very college and university has its own private
scholarship funds which are available only to
students who are attending that particular school.
They are not connected to government grants and
loans, although they are often given on the basis of
the Financial Aid Form and the student's degree of
need.

These scholarships, loans and grants are administered by the school on its own behalf or on behalf of a special interest. The scholarship may be the result of a memorial which was created to honor a well-liked teacher, an outstanding student or a community leader who was active in the affairs of the college. For instance, an endowment could be created to provide tuition assistance to gifted lacrosse players or physically disabled music majors.

Or the scholarship may reflect an emphasis of the college, giving a tuition reduction to children of alumni or certain minorities it wishes to encourage (American Indians or female chemistry majors, for example).

It may be awarded with respect to academic excellence, serving the purpose of enhancing the college's academic reputation by attracting and keeping students with high GPAs. Sometimes it reflects the religious commitment of the school; in a church-related college, children of clergymen in the denomination may receive an automatic reduction in tuition.

One is likely to read in newspapers and magazines that every year millions of dollars of scholarships go unclaimed. Financial aid officers claim this is not the case, but it is true that some school-sponsored scholarships are so specific that it is hard to find any students who meet the qualifications. To wit:

"$526 will be awarded annually to a female student surnamed O'Cohen whose maternal grandfather was an officer in the Spanish-American War and who is attending Ivy League University as a major in Extra-terrestrial Geology with a cumulative Grade Point Average of 3.98 or better, provided such applicant is an orphan with a strawberry birthmark on the right temple."

Contact the financial aid office to obtain more complete information about any private or institutional scholarships for which you may qualify. Knowing about them ahead of time may have a strong influence on where you decide to go to school.

REACH OUT FOR LESS

You're here at school and everyone you want to talk to, *need* to talk to, is suddenly half a continent away. Mom, Dad, Sis, Gramma and Gramps, Woofy, etc.

Don't mope. Ma Bell has a way for you to reach out and touch those you've left behind. But boy, is it expensive! Those long-distance rates are murder!

When you're away the phone is a necessity, but there are ways to cut that phone bill down to size. Follow these simple rules and watch your monthly total shrink before your very eyes.

1 *Make a list.* Before inserting your pinky in the dial, take a couple minutes to jot down a list of all the things you want to talk about. Actually, you can be working on this list all day before your call—it's more fun that way. The list helps you keep from wasting precious seconds while you wrack your brain trying to remember all those things you wanted to tell them back home.

2 *Don't repeat yourself.* They all want to hear what you have to say. But you don't have to go through your list with everyone who grabs the phone to say "hi." Tell each person a new item from your list and that way they can all sit down together and share the news with each other.

3 *Keep a timer by the phone.* Get one of those little hourglass egg timers they use to time a three-minute egg and keep it by the phone. When you call home, start the timer and determine only to turn it two or three times. Even if you lose track of the time, just watching the sand rush through that little glass will make you think of the passing time—and disappearing money—and will help keep conversations brief.

4 *Talk to fewer people.* Sounds callous, but do you really need to talk to little Timmy from down the street just because he's standing there? Or Aunt Sarah who happens to be over for coffee? Talk to one or two people and let them fill everyone else in.

5 *You pick the topics.* Conversation is the give and take of information, of course. But when you call home, it's your nickel; so *you* pick the topics. If long-winded Uncle Ed starts into a thirty-minute expository on the state of trout fishing in Maine, just break in and let him know that you'd love to hear all about it—why doesn't he call you up sometime when you can talk at length? In other words, tactfully

cut short any infringements on your calling time. The phone works two ways. If they have news they can call *you*.

6 *Call after 5.* Better still, call after 11 P.M. if it's not too terribly inconvenient. Phone rates are cheaper after 5, and are usually cheaper still after 11. A prearranged calling time—every Wednesday night at 11:01, for example—will be an event looked forward to and should keep loved ones from worrying when the phone rings late at night.

7 *Save it for the weekend.* Usually rates all day Saturday and until 5:00 P.M. Sunday are at their cheapest (same rate as after 11:00 P.M.) If your news can wait, save it for the weekend when you can have a real gabfest for less.

8 *Don't call, write.* Yes, calling is the next best thing to being there, but you can say a lot in a letter and often say it better. Save phoning for a special treat or when the news just won't wait. The rest of the time, put it down in a letter. Don't forget about electronic mail. To keep charges down, first write it in a word-processing file, then copy and paste it into an e-mail message. Also, try writing a serialized letter. This is one you start in the morning and carry with you all day and work on whenever you have a spare minute and by day's end your epistle will be finished. Be sure to date it—month, day and year—so your folks can save your letters. They'll be good for a cry/laugh in years to come.

BICYCLING

Mindy's Muffins

christmas cards

"The thrill of making a
fast buck follows only
the thrill of love at first
sight. Everyone needs to
take an occasional fling
with money . . . and
with love."

Eliot Janeway

E-N-T-R-E-P-R-E-N-E-U-R

You don't have to know how to
spell entrepreneur to be one. Just
call yourself a tycoon. You are the
type of person who can't get excited

about working in the school library
(shh!) for $1.50 an hour in order to
finance your college education. You
aren't into wearing the same pair of

track shorts all winter long. Fasting is okay, but not for the entire fall semester.

You would like to find an interesting way of making money while in school. You may need it desperately or just want a little more to help grease the wheels of student luxury. You know that you need some experience under your belt once you get out of school ("So tell me, David, what percentage of your college expenses did you earn?"). You think it might be fun to try something different. You like the idea of being more independent—of your parents, the administration, the student loan program.

The following ideas will help get you started. Remember, however, to take into consideration the amount of time you can devote to your venture, your need for a high income vs. a secure income (the library, at least, will pay you what they promise), the campus you're on and your own personal interests.

Be prepared to encounter some administration resistance. There is an anticapitalist prejudice on the part of the academic community generally. (If the question was put to them, they would tell you that *your* job is to *study!*) Some colleges prohibit any kind of moneymaking or fund-raising on campus. Some require approval of the dean (who has yet to give it to anyone) and some have strict regulations that are hard to get around. Some have noncompetition commitments which will prohibit you from taking business away from the food service, student bookstore, campus laundry, etc. At any rate, find out what the restrictions are and live with them until you can persuade the administration to change them—at least in your case.

Susan's Sitting

So without further ado, here are the ideas. The rest is up to you.

1. Students who are studying hard invariably get the munchies before bedtime. Deliver boxes of doughnuts to the lobby of every dormitory (and fraternity and sorority house) at 9:00 each evening. Leave a change box for the students' money. If the total doesn't balance when you come back, that dorm loses its buying privileges. If the honor system proves a persistent problem, post a student to see that nobody filches the goodies. Pay him/her in rolls.

2. Send a snappy promotional letter to students' parents offering to deliver a birthday cake or cram kit (for finals week: crackers, cheese, peanut butter, fruit juice, raisins, cookies, candy, fresh fruit, chips, soft drinks) to their offspring at the appropriate time. Do this as soon as school starts, when they're feeling terrible because Dickie has left home. Based on the number of responses (prepaid, of course), find a supplier and deliver as promised. Cakes can be ordered from a local bakery or you can make them yourself. Cram kits can be assembled all at once from items you have purchased wholesale. Remember that you'll be doing all this work when *you* should be cramming. Your administration can get you a list of parents' names and addresses if it isn't already in the student directory.

3. Become the campus Avon lady, Mary Kay beauty consultant, Amway distributor, Fuller Brush Man or Watkins representative. The products these companies provide are in demand with students. You would be surprised how well-attended a campus Tupperware party can be, too. Check the Yellow Pages for local distributors who can get you started.

4. Be a paper boy. Take subscriptions for the local newspaper, either daily or Sunday delivery. Have your student patrons pay in advance—you don't want to take a chance on their ability to handle credit. Then hire some local kids to do the delivery (you didn't think *you* would be expected to do

all that running around!).

5. Sell Christmas cards. Take orders on behalf of a mail order-type company in November. Deliver the cards the first part of December. You won't make any money if your customers just want one card for Sis and one for Auntie. You will have to sell them on the idea of a mass-mailing; if you're successful, you can make quite a bit of money with the 30 to 50 percent you'll receive on the gross sales. Greeting-card companies carry other types of stationery that are marketable year 'round.

6. Your school has at least two or three major functions every year at which the well-dressed lady will be wearing a corsage: Homecoming, the Snowflake Ball, the Sweetheart Banquet. Most likely the guys in your dorm won't think about flowers until the last minute, if at all. That's where you come in. You can approach your flower sales in one of two ways: 1) Set up a table outside the dining hall or the lobby desk and take advance orders which will be delivered in a timely fashion. 2) Wait until the day of the event and come to the dorm armed with corsages they can buy on the spot (stock white flowers—they go with everything). In either case, arrange ahead of time with a local florist to buy at a discount because of the volume; add an extra dollar or two to compensate for the convenience you are providing for the forgetful male escort. It would be hard to overestimate the need for such a service.

7. Make contact with a local businessman and become his rep on campus to pick up and deliver dry cleaning for a percentage of the take. It could be a big job, but if you're ambitious you can do a twice-weekly laundry gig too.

8. Were you the only one in your high school class who took typing seriously? You say you worked as a secretary for two years before you started back to school? What? You've also got a computer with a neat-o word processing program *and* a laser printer? Wow! You're in luck!

No hardware? Don't despair. You can still make a small fortune typing papers for other students, if you're fast and accurate and can talk the head of the Business School (or Computer Science Department) into letting you come in after classes and use the school's equipment. You provide ribbons and paper, of course.

You can make your services more attractive and make more money by providing extras such as pickup and delivery, proofreading, photocopies, etc.

9. As you sit in *Statistics 302,* glad that you *do* have a math aptitude and you *do* understand how to find the standard deviation and you *do* know when to use the Q-sort approach and you *do* know how to avoid a Type II Error . . . you should also know that you can make big bucks by tutoring those who do not. It is customary for an upperclassman to tutor freshmen, but you can also be of help to those in your own class who just aren't getting it. Either advertise your services on a conspicuous bulletin board or let your professor know that you are willing; he/she may be able to direct you to a needy soul. Or advertise in the community, contacting local elementary and high-school guidance counselors, or advertise in the paper. Tutoring pays well; rates vary somewhat, but you can look for about $10 an hour.

10. Hang out your shingle as the Campus Mover. You will need a small truck (or access to one), a couple of handcarts and perhaps a few friends who throw discus. For a set hourly rate or on the basis of a job estimate you have given, you're going to move other students from the dorm to the frat house, to a new dorm room, to an off-campus apartment or just "out" at the end of the semester. And you're going

to make good money doing it too, because people hate to move and their friends never show up like they say they will and they don't want to haul that Nautilus gym down four flights of stairs alone.

11. Maybe you thought you were through with baby-sitting and maybe you are. Working for a pittance in someone else's home may not cut it for you any more, but consider some new twists to the student's oldest profession. How about a Friday or Saturday night child-care service? You get several of your friends in a good location (house of a family in the community you know, your folks' house if you're living at home, school facilities possibly) and parents can drop their kids off for the evening (consider 6:00 to 12:00) for a fee. It will work best if you charge a set price (say, $6.00 for

FRED'S FOOD
DELIVERY
ROOM SERVICE

TAKE THE BEST—LEAVE THE REST

one child, $10.00 for two per night) no matter how long they leave the child there. If you want to get *really* rich, forego your own party and holiday plans and operate for Homecoming (lots of married students and returning alumni), the Christmas banquet or—this is the biggie, folks—New Year's Eve, 6:00 P.M. to 6:00 A.M. Serve a nutritious snack and plan a "Look what I made for you, Mommy" activity (a crayon drawing will do) and your parent-clients will be impressed and appreciative.

12. With your 35mm. camera you can make a real piece of change (a larger format such as 2¼ or 4 x 5 is better yet). With the right advertising you can be the one they come to for passport and application photos. The college is always needing someone to cover the game, special events, etc. Student organizations need their group photos. Talk to the administration about getting the homecoming concession, taking pictures of every couple as they enter the dance, getting their name and address and a commitment to

buy the picture. Get a deposit, too, if you can. You can negotiate a discount on film and developing from a local vendor if you do all your business with him and it is of sufficient volume.

Now before you hurry off to the bank, there are a few details to think of. If you make very much money, you're going to have to pay income tax; call the local IRS office and ask them for the latest guidelines. If you have employees, you must consider withholding tax, FICA (Social Security tax), unemployment insurance, minimum wage, workers' compensation and overtime. You may decide that it is easier to make it a one-person operation and avoid all that hassle. At any rate, you must keep accurate accounting records of expenses and income. If you are a legal minor (varies from state to state), it may affect your ability to enter into contracts with suppliers; barring this, you may still look like a bad risk because of your youth. And you may need insurance to operate, or a license or permit.

So work at the library if you want, but there's always the possibility that you may find a more interesting way to make it through school by being an entrapanure . . . auntrapenewer . . . entripenneurre . . . untraponner . . . Whatever!

These and scores of other suggestions for making money at your own business are covered in *How to Succeed in Business before Graduating* by Peter M. Sandman and Daniel R. Goldenson—recommended reading!

HIRED OR FIRED

There's gloomy news from the part-time job front: bosses are getting very picky about the people they hire. Competition allows it: with the number of people out looking for jobs, they don't have to hire the first person who comes along.

So how do you land that job? And after you get it, how do you keep it? At grocery stores, restaurants, discount stores and ice cream parlors, we talked to the bosses. "What's the most important thing you look for when hiring a person? What's the secret?" To our surprise there was no big secret. Virtually anyone can get a job, they said, if they follow a few basics. Here are the tips they gave on how to get hired or fired.

HERE'S LOOKING AT YOU— Whoever said appearances are deceiving wasn't a boss. All the bosses we talked to agreed that their first look had the most to do with whether a person was hired or not. The manager of a discount store told us, "I don't expect too much. But when a kid comes in wearing dirty, patched-up jeans and his hair hasn't been washed in a week, that's where I draw the line." Nobody expects an applicant to wear a suit and tie (although you might be hired on the spot if you did), but clean clothes—fresh shirt or blouse and clean jeans—are a must. It's best to avoid fad fashions or ultraflamboyant garb, too. Spend a few minutes in front of the mirror before you go out and ask yourself, "Is what I see what I want the boss to see?"

A TIGER IN YOUR TANK—It's not enough to slouch through the door and mumble, "You don't have any jobs, do you?" An employer likes to see a spark of inner motivation, a little aggressiveness in the people he hires. "A lot of kids don't even bother to come in for an interview—they just call up on the phone," one boss told us. "Those kids haven't got a chance with me." Nothing turns off the boss quicker than a person who won't even stir himself out of his lethargy and shake himself down to interview face to face. The kind of aggressiveness an employer is looking for is easy to show: a firm handshake, an eagerness to learn and enthusiasm to work. That's all.

WATCHOUT!

Most employers you will work for are decent sorts. But every now and then you get an exploitive boss.

Beware the boss who asks you to perform dangerous duties, who doesn't pay you on time, who involves you in anything illegal, or who harasses you.

You may be a student, but you have rights! Report bad bosses to the authorities—the Work Study Coordinator, the Equal Opportunity Commission, the Occupational Safety & Health Administration, or a lawyer.

BEAT THE CLOCK—Part-time jobs are scheduled around the work to be done, not the workers' convenience. Employers are looking for people who will work into any schedule they need filled. It really doesn't make sense to go looking for a job unless you

actually plan to work a regular number of hours a week. A Baskin-Robbins manager told us, "Kids come in who can work two or three hours a week, or only want evenings and no weekends. It's impossible to plan a schedule around people like that." Of course, there are going to be conflicts with classes and other outside interests, and employers understand that. But you've got to meet them halfway. A boss must know if he can count on you to work when you say you will. Is that so much to ask?

ON YOUR OWN TWO FEET— At interview time, a boss will be looking at you closely to determine your RQ (responsibility quotient). If you can show him even a faint glimmer of responsibility—that you can be trusted to carry out your job without constant supervision— he'll probably jump out of his socks. To find out how responsible a new applicant is, he may ask questions like, "Why do you want to work?" or "Why should I hire you?" Those questions can be tough if you haven't thought about them before. So think about it—why *should* anyone hire you? What do you have to offer? Your answer may get you the job.

SIGNING ON THE DOTTED LINE—The rock-bottom basic requirement for any job is the application. We all know applications are a pain, but employers insist on using them. So if you're going to play the game, then get used to filling out endless forms. Before you even think about going in to apply for a job, get a good working ball-point pen and a list of all the addresses and phone numbers you'll need to complete the application. Know your Social Security number. The applications generally follow a standard form—so if you've seen one, you've seen them all. Neatness counts. After a busy day, when the boss is going through the stack of applications to fill an opening, which paper will catch his eyes—the one he can't even read or doesn't list a phone number? Never. (Another good tip is to wait around after you've filled it out and give it to the employer in person.)

MIND GAMES—The chief cause of an employee getting canned is a rotten attitude toward the job. A lot of jobs are boring, low-paying and dirty, but a bad attitude only makes them worse. Contrary to what most students think, employers *do* know when a job is tough. They are more than willing to listen to your suggestions and gripes, as long as they are founded on something more than a reflection of your own bad attitude. You'll run smack into trouble if you start thinking your work is "beneath" you. That happened to one young worker who refused to clean out the kitchen's grease trap. "I'll never do that. It's too dirty," he announced. He was promptly dismissed. That kind of attitude not only affects the way you work, it also affects those around you; and bosses won't tolerate it.

Christmas break can be a great time to make some extra cash: most stores hire plenty of holiday help and also offer employee discounts. But the week between Christmas and New Year's Day is also a time for many conferences and evangelistic projects. Ask your pastor or priest, consult a campus fellowship staff member or chaplain, and surf the World Wide Web for ideas. Among the offerings you'll find denominational conferences, career-geared symposia, Campus Crusade's winter break projects, and InterVarsity's Urbana missions convention (held every three years).

BACKTALK—Any form of fighting, talking back, mutiny-rousing or defiance on the job is usually met with stern action. You owe it to your boss to follow his instructions without talking back (no matter what you may think of him personally). If the boss is clearly at fault, but won't change and won't listen to calm, objective reason, by all means quit. But you can't get away with smarting off to him without paying the penalty.

A THIEF AMONG US—It's a shame to bring this up, but the employers we talked to insisted. So much pilferage occurs by employees that management must take a hard line on the guilty culprits. Swiping merchandise, fudging orders and, as several managers mentioned, giving products away to friends are the usual forms of on-the-job thievery. The standard excuse, "Everyone else does it," just won't cut it when you're caught. Keep yourself clean and you'll keep your job.

SKIPPING OUT—Once you've been hired and agreed to work, you're obligated to show up at the right time, on time. Sure, things come up, but let an employer know as soon as possible when you can't be there. He'll appreciate your thoughtfulness all the more. Some bosses, in a fit of anger at being left shorthanded by a worker who just doesn't show up, might fire a person they really like. You just don't leave them a choice when you force them to be the bad guys. The same goes for being on time—arrive on the job ready to work. Do that consistently and your boss will be impressed.

BOMBS AWAY—Generally, mistakes aren't enough to get you fired. Most employers are tolerant toward errors made on the job: mistakes in making change, mixing up orders, spilling food, losing or breaking tools,

etc. It's when the mistakes get repeated over and over that they get nervous and think about letting the employee go elsewhere. Repeated mistakes indicate that an employee isn't paying attention to what he's doing or that he doesn't care. Don't cover a mistake by lying or weaseling out of the blame, either. Admit your mistakes and make an effort to do better. (If you do continue making mistakes, at least try some new ones.)

TEN DO'S AND DON'TS FOR MAKING YOUR BOSS GLAD HE HIRED YOU

—Do your best always, even in the minor details.
—Don't talk about your boss behind his back.
—Do show up ready for work, on time and on the days you agreed to work.
—Don't hang out with friends who drop by while you're working.
—Do ask questions whenever necessary.
—Don't bring your personal problems to work with you.
—Do make an effort to get along with fellow-employees.
—Don't lie to your boss or cover up for mistakes.
—Do take responsibility for your work; let your boss know he can trust you.
—Don't take anything for granted or leave anything to chance; when in doubt, double check.

The Class Act 3

CHOOSING THE RIGHT CLASSES

We have already stated that your purpose in attending college is to graduate; furthermore, you want to graduate with good grades. In order to do this, you must pay attention to the classes you choose and take into consideration their academic emphasis, their content, their method of instruction and their method of grading. Especially in larger schools, you may find that you can fulfill a basic requirement—math, say—in a number of different ways by taking any one of several courses. The wise student knows that in order to get the best possible grades you must know how to choose the right classes.

Meet the Man

Before taking a class, meet the professor. He's the one who can give you the straight poop on what to expect. His information will be up-to-date: if he's decided to try a different lecturing technique this semester, that's better information than the rundown you got from your older sister who took his class three years ago. His information will be teacher-specific: that is, you can find out how this particular instructor will be running the microbiology lab as opposed to how the rest of the instructors have been doing it. In taking the time to meet with your prospective

instructor you indicate to him that you are a motivated student. That in itself will enhance your possibilities of getting a good grade.

Do It Again

When you find a prof you "click" with, by all means find out what other classes she teaches and take those too. Several advantages: 1) she will remember your bright, happy face when you show up the second, third, fourth time in a class of hers; 2) she will remember that you did well before, and treat you as though you will do well again, which makes an academic encore probable; 3) you will already know her teaching style and grading methods, and consequently you'll spend less time thinking about those things and more time learning; 4) you will have the opportunity to find in her a mentor, a faculty member who knows you and can help you along, a person who can give you a good, honest recommendation later on.

There's no law that says you have to take each class from a different instructor or that you must suffer through the bad profs as well as enjoy the good ones. *You* are here to graduate with good grades. When you find a professor who can help you reach your goal, latch on and don't let go until you have gotten as many credit hours as possible with that *wonderful* academician.

Know Thyself

A self-awareness of your strengths and weaknesses will help you pick the right classes.

If you . . .	Consider . . .
Write well	a class with many written assignments; with a term paper instead of a final exam.
Speak well	seminar classes, and the opportunity for oral examinations.
Memorize well	a class which wraps up with a nice, big objective exam.
Are practical	lab courses.
Are creative	independent study and classes which require special projects.
Are disciplined	correspondence school or independent study.
Learn through hearing	lecture classes.
Learn through reading	correspondence courses or reading courses which rely heavily on textbooks and assigned material.
Do your best work in the morning	morning classes.
Come alive at night	evening and extension courses.
Learn through doing	lab courses, projects.
Like a small class	a small class.
Like a large class	a large class.

There is really no reason why, if you are oriented toward the printed page, you should suffer through a class which uses no text and provides no opportunity to see what you are supposed to be learning in a written form. It is not a sign of inadequacy if you find it hard to understand what is being said in a lecture; that's just the way you're wired. So *find out* the way you learn best. Take a long look at past experiences when you did well or did poorly, and try your best to match your strengths with the teaching method which will help you assimilate and ultimately demonstrate your knowledge.

A Little Bit of This, A Little Bit of That

When it is possible to do so, vary your load. For starters, see if you can find out what the exam schedule is for each class you plan to take before registering for it. Most schools post an exam schedule at registration. Consult it so you don't end up taking three classes whose finals are all on the same day.

Check to see if the classes you propose to take have labs or if a great deal of reading is involved. You don't really want to have to write a term paper for all five courses you will be taking this semester.

A nice semester's schedule might look like this:

COURSE	CREDIT HOURS	PROFILE
Statistics	3 hrs.	Heavy studying involved
Microbiology	5 hrs.	3 hrs. classwork 4 hrs. laboratory work
American Novel	3 hrs.	Long reading list
Printmaking	3 hrs.	Art class, meeting two afternoons a week
Tennis	1 hr.	Fun and exercise

In this schedule, heavy academic classes (Stats, Micro) have been arranged with an interesting literature course (American Novel) and a fun art class. With tennis to keep this student fit, she's in good shape.

When You Are Stuck

You won't always be able to find a class that is suited to your personality; that is taught by a professor you like; that is offered at a good time of day for you; that will contribute to a well-balanced schedule.

Many times you will need to take a class that doesn't fit your style. In such a case, keep close to the professor—get as much help from her as you can. If the idea of the oral exam at the end of the semester is already giving you hives, ask if she can give you advice, pointers, coaching which will help you do a good job. Perhaps you could submit another project in lieu of the oral. Could she suggest a tutor?

At any rate, do your best. In all likelihood you will be able to have control over *most* of your classes and having one or two that you are stuck with isn't the end of the world. Looking on the positive side, maybe you'll discover something about yourself as you struggle through unfamiliar territory— perhaps you'll find a latent ability to excel in an area you were previously afraid of.

Become an Auditor?

Who would want to audit a class? You have to pay for it, you have to do the work, but you don't get the credit. What's the point?

When a class is vital to your academic career and a superior grade is absolutely essential, it is often a good idea to audit the class before taking it for credit so you go into the grading situation with a knowledge of what the material is and what you will be expected to play back at semester's end.

This is the *best* reason for auditing a class, but check with the registrar to see if it's allowed in your school. Some colleges will not let a student audit a class which will later be taken for credit.

GETTING IN
GETTING OUT

What Is a Gut?

Ah, the gut—the class that promises an "A" to any student with enough initiative to sign up for it. Every college has its guts and there's no reason why you, the most serious of students, shouldn't treat yourself to at least one or two in the course of your college career. They go something like this:

> **Geology 201
> (Rocks for Jocks)
> Textile Crafts 220
> (Needlepoint and Basket Weaving, folks)
> General Arithmetic 101
> (Micky Math)
> Children's Literature 202
> (Kiddy Lit)**

Plan ahead; guts get to be well-known on campus and generally fill up quickly.

You study the course descriptions in the catalog, pore over the class schedule, and design the perfect semester—you balance requirements with electives and build a gorgeous course load: *English Composition* at 9:00, M-F. *Biology 101* at 10:00 MWF with the brilliant Dr. Andersen. *The Madonna in Renaissance Art* at 10:00 TTh. *Aerobic Dance* at 11:30 MWF. Beautiful.

So you stand in line with all the other freshmen on the third day of registration (after the sophomores, juniors, and seniors have picked things over). You rush to your stations to pick up cards.

"Sorry, full." "You can't take *The Madonna in Renaissance Art* without *Art Appreciation.*"

"Yes, *Aerobic Dance* is full, too. We can give you *Biology 101* with another professor at another time."

You hurriedly consult the schedule again, looking back and forth to the "full classes" board, then punt. You leave registration two and a half hours later with *English Comp* pretty much as you wanted it, *Biology 101* at 4:30 in the afternoon with some professor called "Staff," a general P.E. class at 8:00 in the morning, and *Music Theory* on Tuesday night at 7:30.

Why did this happen to you? Because you believed the bespectacled lady behind the desk who said, "*PoliSci 201: Political Parties* is full," and "you need *PoliSci 114: American Systems of Government* in order to take

PoliSci 304 and you don't have it; that means you must take *PoliSci 201* as a prerequisite."

ENGLISH 198: *Self-Reliance in a Technological Society. Theory and Practice of Self-Reliance in Today's World.* **In addition to reading and discussing concepts of self-reliance as reflected in literature, students will become members of a legally registered corporation set up just for this class. As members of the corporation they will get a bank loan, purchase a run-down wreck of a house near the university, work on redesigning and remodeling the house, then sell the house and divide the profits. Not for cowards or cleanliness freaks. Both men and women welcome. Enrollment limited to fifteen students. Four credit hours.**

Lehigh University List of Courses, 1976 (Quoted in *The Three Boxes of Life* by Richard Nelson Bolles)

And It Gets Worse!

Well, you have no choice but to attend the classes you chose(!) and make the best of it. So you get to *Biology 101* and find out that "Staff" means "graduate student" and the woman doing the lectures is inaudible, for starters, and so scared to get up and speak that she skips important information and is so glad to get interrupted by a question—any question—that the class period is more often than not spent in meaningless digressions from material that you're going to be tested on.

You may believe that when you find yourself in such a class you are obliged to bite the bullet and finish the semester no matter what kind of horrible grade you will get.

Not so! You have a secret weapon to combat the system. But you have to know what you're up against.

Know the Enemy

Begin by understanding why it is that class size is limited. In the case of a large lecture-survey class it may be because there are only so many seats in the hall. In the case of smaller seminars, it is probably because Prof. Dipstick feels that twenty-four is the optimum number of students for his class, and he thinks that the twenty-fifth student will hinder the progress of the class more than help.

Prerequisites? Just a way of insuring that the students who spend a semester tackling counseling techniques have an inkling of psychological theory on which to base their work. That doesn't mean that if Sigmund Freud wanted to take *Psych 435* he would be excluded because he didn't have *Psych 260*.

Some classes are confined to "majors only" because the faculty available to teach these upper-division courses is limited and the subject matter is of such a specific nature that it probably would not contribute significantly to the academic preparation of students in other fields.

Furthermore, they *will not* have students dropping out of a class just because they don't like the professor or because it's finals time and they know they're not going to make the grade. Class sizes at the end of the term must have some resemblance to the enrollment at the beginning of the term.

So now you know.

Some Good Advice

You can make it easier on yourself by immediately beginning a practice that most students don't catch on to until their senior year, and some not ever. *Always register for one more class than you intend on taking.* Initially, this will give you a heavy course load—eighteen hours when you only want fifteen, for example. Attend all your classes for a week or two. Then, on the last day that you can drop classes and still receive a full tuition refund, ditch the class that you don't want: the class with the incredible syllabus of books that even Evelyn Wood couldn't read; the class with Professor Curmudgeon who is living his life somewhere between the Outer Limits and the Twilight Zone; the class that is full of pre-med majors who are going to study at least sixteen hours a day and mess up the grading curve.

There is really no surer way to see if you'll do well and learn from the course than to attend class. With that one extra class, you are already starting to get control of the situation.

When to take a course pass-fail:

1. When it's mid-term and obvious that you won't get the "A" you need, but you will pass and you don't want to drop out and waste the time and effort you've put in so far.

2. When you want to explore a class outside your major and don't want your GPA to suffer for your adventure.

3. When you have a heavy course load and want at least one class that you can sluff off on, if necessary.

When not to take a course pass-fail:

1. When you might fail.

2. When it's an important class in your major field.

3. When you think you might be transferring to another school. Classes taken pass-fail often do not transfer.

Tactics

Now that you know the reasoning behind the rules, it's time to see what you can do about it.

Picture this: you're in the registration line and find that the class you want is full. This is merely information, not the kiss of death for your plans to take *Anthropology 420: American Indians I Have Known.* Find Professor Dudley, and quick. Search him out, wherever he may be. Let him know that his class is full (at this early date it may be news even to him) and give him your reason for wanting his special permission to take it.

> "I came to Stinky U for the very reason that I wished to study the foraging practices of Northern Plains Indians under you, Professor Dudley. I am now a sophomore and have been unable up to this point to make it into even one of your highly-regarded anthropology classes. I am beginning to question my decision to come to this school at all . . ."

Even the exciting and stimulating Professor Dudley has had enough students over the years who were deadbeats and dullards that he is bound to reconsider his original figure of fifteen as the ideal class size and contemplate sixteen when he realizes who the extra person will be: you, an eager up-and-comer.

You will *not* impress him if you tell him you *need* his class to graduate (especially if you're a freshman) or that it is more convenient than the afternoon section because that's when you watch "General Hospital" or that you can avoid having to take summer school if he'll just be a dear and let you in.

If he insists that the class size stay at fifteen, ask if you may sit in on the class for a week or so in anticipation that one of his students may (regrettably) have to drop the course, creating a vacancy you might fill.

It is the professor—not your advisor or the registrar or the Dean of Students—who determines how many will be in his class. So when

Dudley gives approval, you're in. Take whatever authorization he has given you, hightail it back to the registration and finish the paperwork. Try not to look too smug.

If you lack the required prerequisite for the class you wish to take, the procedure is pretty much the same, except that you will know in advance that you are going to need special permission to get in. Do your pleading with the instructor *prior* to registration. Again, it is the instructor who has jurisdiction over who gets into her class. She can waive the prerequisite, once convinced that your experience as a street artist in San Francisco last summer doing caricatures of tourists is ample preparation for *Drawing from Life*.

If it's a class for majors only, explain why the course is important to you: that although you are a psychology major, you are planning on getting a job in personnel after you graduate. For this reason, you need to take *Labor Economics* as background for understanding union negotiations and relations. Keeping in mind that most professors love to proselytize for their department, a hint that you are thinking of changing your major from Animal Husbandry to Dramatic Arts could be very persuasive.

Be assertive but not obnoxious. You don't want to be remembered as the nuisance who made a bother of herself by pleading and pleading, and then cried when she didn't get her way. You want to be an exception to the rule, but there are times when you may have to accept "no" graciously and live with the decision.

Getting Out

Now you know how to get into a class; there are times when it is just as important to know how (and when) to get out. On the whole, you will find the administration and faculty less interested in the courses you drop than the ones you keep.

There are several good reasons to drop a class, among them that—

1. You took more hours than you wanted and now you're making your final decision.

2. You are not academically prepared to get a good grade in the class.

3. You sense a personality conflict between yourself and the instructor which will adversely affect your ability to learn anything and/or earn a good grade.

4. You misjudged the scope of the class and believe that the subject, as it is being taught, is not a good use of time and money.

5. You just do not, for one reason or another, like the class.

If you went through all sorts of inspired machinations to get into the class it's going to be embarrassing to drop it since you will invariably be required to get drop approval from the same person you pleaded with to take the course. Not to worry. Just tell Professor Dudley,

"I am sorry to impose on you once again, but after attending your class for three weeks I now see that I need to do some supplemental reading on my own to come up to the preparedness level of the other students who are taking *American Indians I Have Known.* Would you please initial this . . ."

You may not need to see him at all. Perhaps a short trip to the registrar's office will solve the problem—so much the better. Check the catalog for the exact procedure.

Pay attention to your school's policy on dropping courses as it affects tuition refunds, financial aid and what will be recorded on your transcript (WP—"Withdrew Passing" vs. WF—"Withdrew Failing"). To a prospective employer, a lot of dropped classes will make you look like the kind of person who bugs out at the first sign of trouble.

The Big Picture

Your goal is to have a good experience while in college, but more than that *you want to graduate.* You want a nice, clean transcript, full of good grades in the right courses. You should not allow yourself to be bullied or intimidated into taking classes you can't use, and then getting poor grades in them. The college exists to educate you—take charge and get the education you came for.

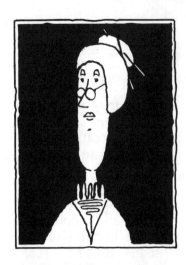

PROFESSORIAL PROTOTYPES

You see them roaming the halls between classes, and holding court in the coffee shop—the professors, absolute monarchs of their tiny classroom kingdoms. Although all are individuals in their own right, as instructors they can usually be classified under certain general categories.

 ## Herr Scholar

While he may not insist on actually wearing his doctoral robes to class, he does clothe himself in an air of erudite sophistication three layers thick. You may call him "Dr. Scholar" or "Dr. Scholar, sir." His lectern becomes a podium in the Hall of Wisdom where he condescends to utter his gems of knowledge for the benefit of lesser mortals, his students.

His command of the subject is formidable, his tongue sharper than a two-edged scalpel. Do not put forth an original idea in his class or you will be cut down to the size of a postage stamp in less time than it takes to say, "Ishouldakeptmybigmouthshut!"

His Eminence does not fraternize

with the lowly student, but rather looks upon them as the one regrettable flaw in a near-perfect profession. He does not invite student participation, though he recognizes talent and will reward it. Do your work well and you'll be treated fairly. Remember that in his class you will learn *his* way.

Instructor Buddy McBuddy

Light years away from Herr Scholar is the first- or second-year instructor who is the student's best friend. He's a regular Joe Cool: smokes in the classroom, goes out drinking with the guys on Friday night, knows all the latest light-bulb jokes. For him, life is one continual personality contest and he's the only contestant. He wants you to like him; he *needs* you to like him.

He's a bon vivant, a born funny guy. All the women fall for him and all the men imitate his deadpan delivery. Each of his classes is well attended because at 1:30 on Tuesdays and Thursdays it is *the* place to be. This guy chaperones the Christmas vacation ski trip, is the resident advisor for the most hip men's dorm and hangs out in the student union—not the teacher's lounge.

He doesn't realize, though, that you're not paying for a lounge act—you're paying for an education. He rarely gives assignments and never takes roll. About three weeks before the term is over he gets the guilties and starts loading on the assignments and cramming his lectures with everything he didn't cover all semester. His tests are bears, because even though you haven't covered half of the material in class you'll suddenly be expected to know it.

He may be entertaining, but this instructor gets nothing but bad reviews as a prof.

Professor Relevant

This newly-tenured professor in his mid-forties is going through a mid-life crisis, and you're invited. He meets his estranged wife, a full professor in the Drama Department, for coffee in the Union every morning at 11:00. This is typical of Professor Relevant.

Having spent thirteen years as a straight arrow, his behavior is now erratic and his moods changeable. He is experimenting with his life and teaching style, developing new techniques and toying with all sorts of classroom theatrics. Since they can't fire him, he is down on the whole academic system and spends a good deal of class time insinuating that you are unenlightened by virtue of your presence. If you ask him how you will be graded he dodges and refuses to answer, explaining that grades are irrelevant and unimportant. Then he gives you a C-.

Although his field is biology he expects you to be as attentive to his opinions about the Board of Regents, coed dorms, apartheid and existentialism as you are about ecosystems and frog anatomy. Abuse of influence is the name of the game as he rambles on and on about every topic under the sun. Don't worry, though—he's going on sabbatical next year to try to get his head together while researching fruit bat physiology.

Professor Emeritus

This doddering old lady has been at CSU for forty-eight years. She was the first woman in the state of Connecticut to receive a doctorate in psychology. She has been influential in her field and is a personal friend of Anna Freud. She has at least two earned Ph.D.s and seven honorary degrees from universities all over the world. The administration has named the new lecture hall after her.

She is, however, nearly senile. She teaches only one class each semester, at the only time during the day when she is even semi-alert. She is almost always late to class and dismisses early because she's plum tuckered out. She wears the same blue dress every day (with blue hair to match). It takes about three weeks to learn how to understand her, and an ear horn to hear her. She tends to ramble, poor dear, and often loses her place, giving the same lecture two days in a row.

Listen carefully, though. Lots of what you read in your textbook was pioneered by her. She's not parroting someone else's research or theories—these are original with her. She's a gold mine to the student who is truly interested in her field and work.

And at her age, she's also lost her desire to flunk kids. Courtesy equals an "A" to this *grande dame.*

Dr. Activist

She marched in Selma, organized the moratorium on campus in 1969, and headed up the student strikes in 1971. She has signed photographs in her office of John F. Kennedy, George McGovern, Gloria Steinem and Karl Menninger. She is a member of every socially and politically relevant organization in the country. Last year she went to Nicaragua with Amnesty International to view the situation there. Her office is overflowing with Congressional Registers, special interest newsletters and third-world newspapers.

Students consult her on unfair housing practices by off-campus landlords, draft registration and the lack of minority representation on the student council. She is likely to teach a class on "German Hegemony in Latin America," "Assertiveness Training for Women" or "Civil Liberties in the 1980s." Any of these classes, however, can be expected to eventually disintegrate into a diatribe against the establishment and a call to arms against the administration. Instead of term papers and final exams you have field projects. This is the gal who drops you off on Chicago's South Side Friday night with $2.00 in your pocket and picks you up on Sunday afternoon—if you survive—and expects a paper on it.

She is not for the fainthearted. If you can take it, you'll learn a lot. You can also be assured that there will be no class on Martin Luther King's birthday or Earth Day.

Professor Art Sankrafts

This guy is eccentricity in a salt-and-pepper beard. He wears a corduroy jacket with paint on the lapels and elbows, corduroy pants with paint on the knees, paint-spattered sneakers, and a blue denim tie with—you guessed it—a paint-dipped tip.

He thinks trees are violet, that the human body is a collection of cones and cylinders, that objects are elastic. He has invented a new kind of plastic paint which he makes for his students. He will listen attentively to the most incoherent rubbish—as long as it pertains to the creative experience—and pronounce it profound.

His enthusiasm for experimenting is infectious, his methods of teaching bizarre. He never does the same thing twice. He welcomes the odd, the unusual, the outlandish, the clever, the strange—all with the same benign acceptance. Tell him you find Post-Impressionism stimulating and he's in seventh heaven; tell him you're devoting your life to painting with chopsticks and you've a friend forever.

He's a nut, a looney toon, but if you try to get on his wavelength, see the world as he sees it—at least occasionally—you'll discover a whole realm of images and creative possibilities you never knew existed. In his own way he can cast light into darkened corners, sharpen up dull senses and stimulate even the most latent creative urge.

Associate Professor Realguy

Along with all the misfits and goofballs, the inadequates and unrealistics, there will be a few professors on campus that are dedicated, dependable teachers. Prof. Realguy is in it for the long haul and he's not cutting any corners. His classes are attended by serious students, his lectures are understandable and current, his assignments are relevant and he grades fairly.

He's fixing up an old house near the campus and if you're a friendly and sincere learner you're likely to be invited over some evening with a few other upperclassmen to discuss some tangent issues and drink some good coffee. He brings his wife and kids to basketball games.

He stays after class to answer questions and has evening review sessions before finals. He's easy to get ahold of and will see you in his office even if you haven't made an appointment with his secretary. He understands when you can't get a term paper in because your grandfather died. He's seen enough to recognize a phony excuse, though, and you won't get by on good looks when it comes time to hand out final grades.

He makes you think that you might want to go into teaching someday. After you graduate you can use him for a reference, and he'll give you a good one. When you attend Homecoming, he remembers you.

> **"A teacher who is attempting to teach without inspiring the pupil with a desire to learn is hammering on cold iron."**
>
> Horace Mann

65

Officially Speaking

4

THE
FIVE
RULES
OF
ACADEMICS

I
II
III
IV
V

Professor Marvin Karlins of the University of South Florida almost failed to graduate from high school. He entered the University of Minnesota on academic probation. Four years later he graduated summa cum laude and Phi Beta Kappa and went on to receive his Ph.D. in psychology from Princeton University.

In his book *The Other Way to Better Grades* he presents the following rules which must be followed by a student who wishes to do well in college.

RULE I: YOUR PRIMARY GOAL IN COLLEGE IS TO GRADUATE. An athlete who appreciates the philosophy and history of his sport still has as his main objective to win the game. If you want only to learn, then read on your own and take odd courses as you find them. But if you are in college, it is because you want a degree; you want to graduate. Therefore, choose your college, major and classes with graduating as your primary goal.

RULE II: A COLLEGE IS NOT A SHRINE, IT IS A BUSINESS. DEAL WITH IT THE WAY YOU WOULD WITH ANY OTHER BUSINESS.

Don't let the pomp and circumstance surrounding academia fool you; mainly it serves to reduce public scrutiny of its activities and create a sense of awe in the students so that they will be subservient to the college's wishes. Understanding this important point will give the student greater confidence to act in his own best interest when confronted with a possible mistake, inequity or prejudice on the part of the college faculty or administration.

RULE III: TODAY, MORE THAN EVER BEFORE, COLLEGES NEED YOU TO STAY IN BUSINESS.

It's a buyer's market—and you are the buyer. Due to a smaller number of potential students in the important 18-25 age range and the popularization of alternatives to a regular four-year college program, the schools are generally looking for students and trying to find ways to keep them in—not throw them out. They need your high GPA, your money, your warm body in a desk.

RULE IV: HIGHER EDUCATION FUNCTIONS AS A SYSTEM. YOU CAN GET BETTER GRADES WITHIN THE SYSTEM ONCE YOU RECOGNIZE ITS EXISTENCE AND LEARN HOW IT OPERATES.

You *recognize* the system; you don't necessarily change it—that's the slow, hard way. Like the athlete, the more you know about your opponent the better prepared you'll be. If you fail to graduate, ignorance will be no excuse; it will be the cause.

RULE V: PROFESSORS ARE NOT DEITIES.

Once you realize that professors are not perfect, nor are they equally competent, you'll be in a position to deal with them on a more realistic level—as individuals who differ in skills, temperament and preferences; as factors that should be considered when selecting a course and working toward a grade.

"In education we are striving not to teach youth to make a living, but to make a life."

William Allen White

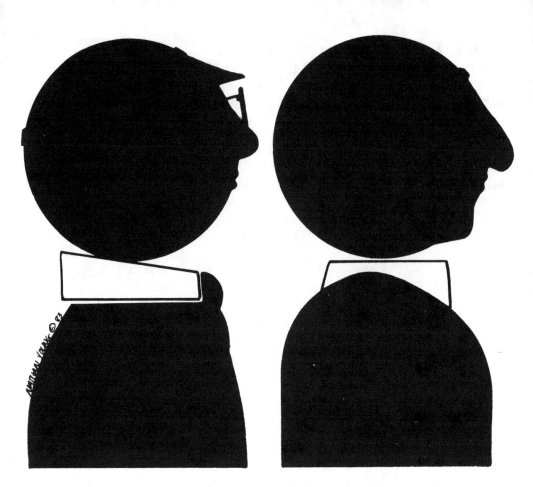

You were a junior in high school before you found out who the administrative vice-principal was; will you be a junior in college before you discover who the academic dean is, or what he does? There are buildings filled with offices and secretaries, there are certain signatures to get on certain forms, there are people to see to get various things accomplished . . . where do you go?

The paid staff at any college or university is divided into two basic groups: administration and faculty. The faculty are those most directly involved in teaching you.

It is to these people that you have entrusted your highly-impressionable mind. They are the ones who stand up in front of you during class, who test you on your acquired knowledge and decide your grades. The class schedule won't tell you, but some have more clout and experience than others. They are not all created equal.

Instructor: He's the rookie, the low man on the totem pole. Perhaps he's a Ph.D., but it's not likely. This is his first year teaching. He usually lacks an advanced degree—we hope he's working on it. Many times his

WHO'S WHO

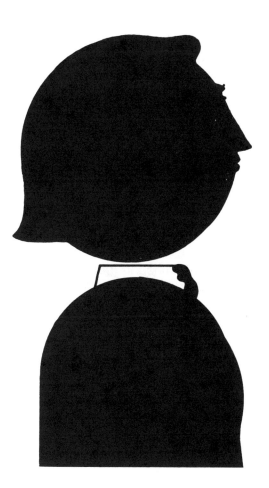

position with the school is temporary—he's teaching until he can get into research at Massachusetts General. He may be a graduate student who has been put on staff. This doesn't mean he isn't a dynamite teacher or a supremely gifted academician. It just means that the college has its standards and this is where he sits.

Assistant professor: She's more likely to have her doctorate than an instructor. Many times this position is the entry-level for a Ph.D., and she'll stay here for a few years while she acquires seniority. She does not have

tenure—the ultimate vote of confidence which is bestowed upon senior professors, insuring that they can stay on staff just about as long as they like (their dismissal being allowed only on the basis of gross misconduct of one kind or another).

Associate professor: The only one who will associate with a professor (old college joke; heh, heh). Once an assistant professor has been given tenure, he's bumped up to associate professor. Now he's got it made. He can relax and practice that academic freedom he's heard so much about all his life. He's a solid part of the university.

Professor: They're all going for full professor. It's the highest rank one can achieve without having any administrative duties. To achieve full professor, he must have been at the school for a specified number of years, have the doctoral degree appropriate to his field and have tenure.

Major professor: This senior guy is one who is involved in directing a graduate student's research. Some schools don't make this distinction (because they don't have a graduate school, maybe).

Department chairman: Where they take a great professor and decide that she's the best in the department, so they make her chairman which means that she has a lot of meetings to go to and a lot of faculty members to review and a lot of new textbooks to check out and a lot of correspondence to handle. So where's she going to find time to teach? She only teaches one or two classes a term, so there you are.

The administration consists of those people whose primary purpose is to make sure that the school stays in business. Sometimes they are faculty who have been promoted to their highest level of incompetence (The Peter Principle), and sometimes they are career administrators. On the whole, these folks were there long before you came and they'll be there long after you leave. To them the university is like a hotel with people checking in and out

Student: One who learns less and less about more and more until he knows practically nothing about everything.

Teacher: One who learns more and more about less and less until he knows a very great deal about nothing.

Administrator: One who already knows a great deal about nothing, so he learns less and less about less and less and ends up knowing nothing about anything.

all the time. At their worst, they are committed to perpetuating the system so they can keep their jobs until retirement. At their best, they make the school operate efficiently and profitably, leaving the teaching and learning to professors and students, with a view toward enriching student life and furthering the pursuit of knowledge (whew!).

President (sometimes called Chancellor): He is responsible to the Board of Trustees (or the Board of Regents) for the operation of the university. He is in charge, ultimately, of budgeting, fund-raising, student relations, faculty development, et cetera, et cetera. Eventually, any major problem is going to be his monkey and any success is going to be a feather in his cap. In big schools he's practically never seen by the student body. In small colleges he may even teach a class and eat lunch in the cafeteria. He is highly visible to alumni and the community at large and chosen largely for his ability to represent the college favorably.

Vice-presidents (sometimes called Vice-chancellors): These folks are responsible for specific areas such as development (getting endowments and financial support for the school); academic affairs (curriculum content and faculty matters); student affairs (housing, sports programs, student union activities); admissions (recruiting desirable students, maintaining requirements for admission to the school). The exact titles and duties vary from college to college and university to university.

Deans: In your school you may not have vice-presidents and such, just a bunch of deans who are in charge of academic affairs, student affairs, etc. In some large universities, each separate college will have a dean in charge of that college, such as the Dean of the Dental School or Dean of the Business School.

When it comes to deans, the possibilities are nearly endless. Most times you can find out what's up with these guys by reading all about it in the college catalog.

Bursar: The man with the green eye shade and sleeve garters who collects tuition and fees. And if you don't pay on time he tells the . . .

Registrar: . . . who won't release your grades until you settle your account. The registrar keeps the statistics; he collects all the grades and posts them to your card, keeps your transcript and—for a fee—sends it out to your prospective graduate school or employer after you graduate (before, even). He is an authority on all matters academic (such as which credits will transfer in and out and which ones won't) and a good friend to have. He rarely makes mistakes, but you'll want to watch out just the same.

Maintenance and security: Call maintenance if your room doesn't have any heat; call security if you're locked out of your freezing room. By the way, it's security that issues parking tickets and puts a "boot" on your car so you can't drive when you get ten tickets in one semester.

The titles and positions may vary from one campus to another. By all means, find out what the titles are on your campus and find out who the people are who occupy these slots. While we're on the subject, there is one more position you should know—the student!

Ultimately, you are the star of the show. If you, the student, aren't there, college is a house of cards that collapses. Many administrators and faculty (especially your professors who are heavy into research or ego or both) do not practice this truth on a day-to-day basis, but it's fact and if you have to remind them, that's okay. They all serve *you;* their highest call is to make sure that college does its job in making you an educated person.

STATUTES OF STUDENT LIMITATIONS

Every college has its rules. At a large state university they are few; at a small church-sponsored college they may be many. Some schools regulate what students wear or length of hair (yes, even in this enlightened age) and chaperone virtually every contact between members of the opposite sex (don't laugh—it's true!).

Contrary to popular opinion, the rules governing student life are *not* laid down to make you miserable. They are given by ordinarily benevolent college officials to 1) promote a healthy atmosphere where learning can take place, 2) protect the rights of individual students— presumably those who come to college to actually learn something, 3) smooth the often rough road of social interaction between students of differing life-styles and backgrounds and 4) help keep worried parents from calling up the dean every few days.

That being the case, rules are a fact of college life. There is no escape. It therefore behooves students to come to grips with this dark reality and make peace with it. Toward this end, we've constructed a four-point peace plan that will, if taken to heart, make adjusting easier.

ONE

Learn the rules ahead of time— Don't wait until you get on campus to discover what the rules are; find out before you enroll. This will help minimize the shock and will give you time to decide whether you can live with them comfortably for the next few years.

If you think the rules are too restrictive *before* you get on campus, imagine what you'll feel like once you're there! It's best to find out early what will be expected of you; it could save you a lot of grief. If you think you can't live with the rules, don't go to that school.

TWO

Conform—happily—Grudging compliance is frowned upon by the administration; it won't win any friends. Often it is not enough to just go along with the rules—you must enjoy it. If that strikes you as pushing the limits of goodwill, consider this: we know of one actual case where a student was expelled not for disobeying the rules but for obeying them with a dubious attitude. The school felt that her questionable disposition encouraged other students to nuture improper attitudes also. *The Rules Will Not Be Mocked!* You'll find that a popular song among college officials.

THREE

Avoid the smorgasbord approach— Many students simply pick and choose among the rules, obeying the ones they feel okay about and ignoring the ones they disagree with. There is no surer way to bring the hot coals of academic disapprobation down on your shiny head. Once you're caught in an infraction, your whole character and personal integrity is called into question. You'll be a marked target. All the rules apply equally to all students. The least you can do is to do your own small part in obeying them; it makes it easier on everybody.

Here again, that might seem a hard line, but we know of an instance where one student broke a rule and was promptly dismissed from school. Her three suitemates were also dismissed even though they had committed no infraction. They were bounced because the school felt that since they all knew the rules they all should have helped each other obey them. It didn't matter that they all obeyed every other rule; the one broken was enough to blotch four otherwise spotless records.

FOUR

*Don't expect change—*Many students refuse to take the rules seriously. "These went out with the dinosaurs and nickel Cokes!" they shout. "We'll soon get things up-to-date." Famous last words.

The reality is that

administrations and their rules are in for the long haul—they plan on being around to give *your* children an education, and your grandchildren, etc. You the student, on the other hand, are around for a scant four years at most—a mere blink of the educational eye, so to speak. How you feel about the rules means very little to them. After all, why should they change them for you when you're just passing through rapidly on your way to somewhere else?

It's true that once in every great while the administration will take pity on the thousands of voices petitioning for a change and actually loosen up on a regulation or two. But you should not count on it happening in your lifetime— at least not in your term of office as a student. It's okay to lend your effort to ease restrictions you feel are unfair or out-of-date; just don't expect it to happen. Rules change, but rarely.

If you're thinking this peace plan is pessimistic, you're right—to a certain extent. It is a slap of sobering reality. Too many students come to college thinking "nine-month holiday" only to find it feels more like a stretch in a Russian work camp. Most students adjust to the rules easily but for those who do not there's no use in chafing yourself raw under an unnecessary harness. It would be better for you and everyone else to go somewhere else.

WHAT THE PROFESSOR REALLY MEANS*

by J. Timothy Petersik

What the prof. said:

You'll be using one of the leading textbooks in this field.

If you follow these few simple rules, you'll do fine in the course.

The *gist* of what the author is saying is what's most important.

Various authorities agree that . . .

The answer to your question is beyond the scope of this class.

What it means:

I used it as a grad student.

If you don't need any sleep, you'll do fine in the course.

I don't understand the details either.

My hunch is that . . .

I don't know.

You'll have to see me during my office hours for a thorough answer to your question.	I don't know.
In answer to your question, you must recognize that there are several disparate points of view.	I really *don't know.*
Today we are going to discuss a most important topic.	Today we are going to discuss my dissertation.
Unfortunately, we haven't the time to consider all of the people who made contributions to this field.	I disagree with what roughly half of the people in this field have said.
We can continue this discussion outside of class.	1. I'm tired of this—let's quit. 2. You're winning the argument—let's quit.
Today we'll let a member of the class lead the discussion. It will be a good educational experience.	I stayed out too late last night and didn't have time to prepare a lecture.
Any questions?	I'm ready to let you go.
The implications of this study are clear.	I don't know what it means, either, but there'll be a question about it on the test.
The test will be fifty-question multiple choice.	The test will be sixty-question multiple guess, plus three short-answer questions (one thousand words or more).
The test scores were generally good.	Some of you managed a B.
The test scores were a little below my expectations.	Where was the party last night?
Some of you could have done better.	Everyone flunked.
Before we begin the lecture for today, are there any questions about the previous material?	Has anyone opened the book yet?
According to my sources . . .	According to the guy who taught this class last year . . .
It's been very rewarding to teach this class.	I hope they find someone else to teach it next year.

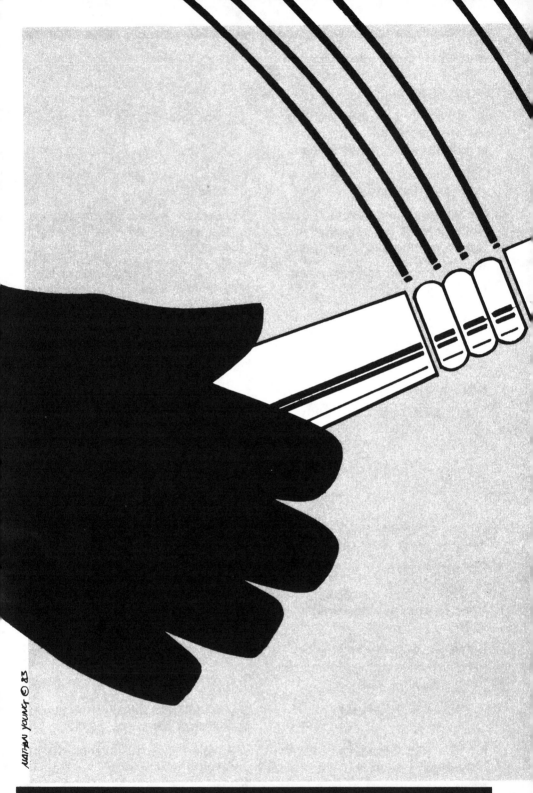

THE CASE FOR STUDENT RIGHTS

• A large state university had a student union building whose facilities were made available to over 100 campus clubs for their meetings. A religious group on campus wanted to use one of the rooms on a regular basis for their Bible studies and prayer meetings. The university wouldn't allow it, claiming that the school would be put in a position of providing "support to an institution of religion," and would not be upholding separation of church and state.

• At a certain Christian college dating between black and white students is forbidden. School officials maintain that this policy reflects the theological views of the college. The American Civil Liberties Union maintains that such a policy is contrary to the constitutional rights of the students as expressed in the Constitution and federal law, and since the college receives tax-exempt status and its students are the recipients of government-sponsored loans and grants the university is breaking the law by prohibiting interracial dating. Therefore, they must either allow the dating or forfeit their favored tax status. School officials claim that freedom of religion is threatened if they cannot create and enforce their own doctrinally-based policies.

• Richard is a twenty-year-old college junior who is required to live in on-campus housing. The school maintains that living in the residence hall is an integral part of the college experience which they provide; that it facilitates important social interactions and a community of scholarship which contributes to his education overall. Richard maintains that 1) he is of legal age and should be able to choose his place of residence and 2) the college has been unwilling and/or unable to concretely demonstrate that living in the residence hall serves any other purpose than merely to fill the dormitory with paying customers.

• At a small, church-related school male students who have achieved sophomore status are not subject to "hours"; that is, they need not be back in the dorm at any particular time of night. Female students, however, live with a curfew from their freshman year until they graduate. At the same time, this school presents a statement on all its literature claiming that it does not discriminate on the basis of "race, sex, national origin." It receives federal and state financial support in the form of student loans and grants, and tax-exempt status.

• Elaine lived with her parents in a state where the age of majority is twenty-one. She now attends school in a state where the legal age is eighteen. As a nineteen-year-old, she went to the student health service of the university and arranged for some minor surgery to be performed there. Is she legally capable of signing the surgical consent forms on her own or, as a resident of the state with a higher age limit, must she get her parent's signature on the consent form? Furthermore, can she demand that her parents not be notified of the surgery? After all, she lives in a state where she is recognized as an adult. Why do her parents have to know what happened?

What a can of worms! All of the preceding cases are based on actual situations involving legal and constitutional rights of students. And none of them (except the case of the religious group that wanted to use the student union) have been resolved (the court found for the group). What was once accepted as the normal function of a college or university's jurisdiction over its students is now being challenged in the courts and before policy-making committees of schools all over the country. Even at church-affiliated schools—who once considered themselves exempt from any such investigation—students, parents and legal advocacy groups are questioning the right of an academic institution to enforce restrictions on students' private lives.

Prior to World War II, most students who attended colleges and universities did so immediately after graduating from high school. They attended college for four straight years and then left; very often they graduated only a short time after reaching the age of majority—twenty-one. After WWII, partly due to the creation of the G.I. Bill and the interruption that the war caused in many students' educational pursuits, a larger number of older students began to populate the nation's college campuses. And in 1971 an amendment was passed to the Constitution—the Twenty-sixth Amendment—which stated that voting rights would be extended to the 18-21 age group. This was the impetus needed to have nearly every state legislature which had not already done so enact laws lowering the age of majority from twenty-one to either eighteen or nineteen. That action gave new rights to many students. And it has affected many areas of academic policy.

"Education makes a people easy to lead, but difficult to drive; easy to govern, but impossible to enslave."

Attributed to Lord Brougham

There may come a time while you are in school that you will question seriously a policy of the school in light of what you believe to be your constitutional rights. Perhaps the policy you question is one having a significant impact on your life; perhaps you are interested in it for purely ideological reasons. (For example, I was a student at a college that had "unequal" hours for men and women students. Although I was a married student living off campus I was bothered by the unfairness of the rule—even though it didn't affect me directly.) Maybe you don't care about the policy one way or the other but can't resist the opportunity to make waves. Any of these reasons has *some* degree of validity, and if you are interested in investigating a school's policy or practice with a view toward changing it to be more fair and just, you might consider the following:

1. Understand that you may make a lot of enemies with the faculty, administration and student body by rocking the boat. If you are successful in effecting change, they will be humiliated; if you are unsuccessful, they will gloat. Either way, your name will probably be mud.

2. Check the student handbook and all other policy statements you can get your hands on to make sure you understand the school's expressed stance on the issue. Compare what you find there to what is actually happening. Make sure you have your facts straight. Do not accept hearsay as evidence; verify all sources. If you are the victim of an unfair policy talk to friends about it to make sure that you aren't just reacting in anger to something that is perfectly fair, perfectly legitimate.

3. Begin by presenting your case to the appropriate administrative office. Be well-prepared, cool-headed, and polite as you explain your position. An example:

"Dean Winter, I have been looking through the student handbook and I checked with the housing office, and I think I see a problem with this rule against having refrigerators in the dorm rooms. As long as I have a full meal ticket (not taking business away from the food service) and the refrigerator is approved by Underwriter's Laboratories (making it safe—safer than popcorn poppers, which *are* allowed) and I have the type of refrigerator which can be plugged into any 110 outlet and I

> ## "There is no crisis to which academics will not respond with a seminar."
>
> Marvin Bressler

don't keep beer or anything like *that* in it, I really don't see what possible reason you could have for disallowing their use. I did a little checking and found out that PYU used to have a similar proscription, but they lifted the ban six years ago. Isn't this a policy that could be reconsidered?"

4. If your well-stated case falls on deaf ears, keep going up the ladder. You can find out the path of power in the handbook or from the first person you talked with (in this case, Dean Winter). This may involve petitioning a committee or presenting your case at the next meeting of the Board of Trustees. If you can't wait for the Board to meet (since your situation is urgent), or you are still unsuccessful in convincing the administration (and you remain firm in your belief), the next step would be to . . .

5. Begin court litigation. This is not fun and games. We do not suggest this except in the most *crucial* of situations. For example, we would not recommend that you take the school to court over the refrigerator issue. But if you have been suspended from school without due process or if you are prevented from exercising your civil rights—such as freedom of

religion—you may be justified in disregarding personal popularity and comfort to make sure the issue is resolved—for yourself and for other students.

On education: "One of the few things a person is willing to pay for and not get."

William Lowe Bryan

Assuming that your financial resources are limited, we would suggest contacting the American Civil Liberties Union in your area or some other advocacy group. They will be able to tell you if your complaint is appropriate, if litigation is feasible and what steps must be taken. Initially, they will contact the school with your complaint. Often this is all that is needed to get the administration's serious attention to a policy that may be unfair or unconstitutional. If that doesn't work, then they will file suit and take the school to court. If you are victorious in court, the judge will order the school to take certain steps to come into line with the decision. The school may appeal the decision, which could further delay any change. If you fail to convince the court, you can appeal too.

As you can see, it's a messy thing to try to change a school policy. It's not for the weak, it's not for those who are easily discouraged, and it's not for misguided do-gooders.

Some universities sincerely want to be brought into line with current legal interpretations, and will be very receptive to change.

"I see your point, Jim. If the Gay Students Task Force gets to meet at the Union, there's no reason why your group shouldn't be extended the same right. I'll talk to Mr. Dickens and get that cleared up."

Some universities, however, resent the recent rulings and laws that have stripped them of some authority and given students greater freedom than they believe students deserve.

"Absolutely not. It is the firm belief of the Board of Regents, the Office on Student Affairs and myself that women should not be allowed to compete in any contact sports which are supported by this school. And we'll hear no more of that kind of nonsense! You are free to participate in the women's intramural tennis league or jog around campus in your spare time but . . ."

Deciding whether or not to work for change is up to you, up to your good sense and discretion. If you came to school knowing what the restrictions were, knowing what would be expected of you and now you start acting like the Ralph Nader of the freshman class, you're in for trouble. Most likely your appeals will be ignored by administration and courts alike. If, on the other hand, the administration is conducting affairs contrary to its stated policy or if you find that your constitutional rights are being trampled underfoot you have a good chance of effecting a change for the better.

Making the Grade

5

EXAM WEEK PREVIEW

Instructions: Read each question carefully. Answer all questions. Time limit—four hours. Begin immediately.

Public Speaking: 2,000 riot-crazed aborigines are storming the classroom. Calm them. You may use any ancient language except Latin or Greek.

Music: Write a piano concerto. Orchestrate and perform it with flute and drum. You will find a piano under your seat.

Psychology: Based on your knowledge of their works, evaluate the emotional stability, degree of adjustment and repressed frustrations of each of the following: Alexander of Aphrodisias, Rameses II, Gregory of Nicea, Hammurabi. Support your evaluation with quotations from each man's work, making appropriate references. It is not necessary to translate.

Engineering: The disassembled parts of a high-powered rifle have been placed in a box on your desk. You will also find an instruction manual printed in Swahili. In ten minutes a hungry Bengal tiger will be admitted to the room. Take whatever action you feel appropriate. Be prepared to justify your decision.

Economics: Develop a realistic plan for refinancing the national debt. Trace the possible effects of your plan on the following areas: Cubism, the Donatist controversy, the wave theory of light. Outline a method of preventing these effects. Criticize this method from all possible points of view.

Political Science: There is a red telephone on the desk beside you. Start World War III. Report at length on its sociopolitical effects, if any.

Physics: Explain the nature of matter. Include in your answer an evaluation of the impact of the development of mathematics on science.

Philosophy: Sketch the development of human thought; estimate its significance. Compare with the development of any other kind of thought.

History: Describe the history of the papacy from its origins to the present day, concentrating especially, but not exclusively, on its social, political, economical, religious and philosophical impact on Europe, America, Asia and Africa. Be brief but concise.

Biology: Create life. Estimate the differences in subsequent human culture if this form of life had developed 500 million years earlier, with special attention to its probable effect on the English parliamentary system. Prove your thesis.

Epistemology: Take a position for or against truth. Prove the validity of your position.

Medicine: You have been provided with a razor blade, a piece of gauze and a bottle of alcohol. Remove your appendix. Do not suture until your work has been inspected. You have fifteen minutes.

Theology: Define the "historical position" of the Lutheran Church—Missouri Synod in twenty-five words or less.

General Knowledge: Define the universe; give three examples.

TAKING AN EXAM:

GET READY, GET SET, GO!

It's kind of like a race, see? You train, you prepare, knowing the challenge you face. No one cares how you looked in practice; now you're under the gun. And a lot of things can go wrong on the track: maybe it rained the night before, maybe you get a cramp in the second lap, maybe you aren't able to psych yourself up for the big finish.

That's often the way it is when you are facing a mid-term, a final or even a weekly German vocabulary quiz. The following suggestions and pointers will help you do as well as you possibly can on the next test you take.

GET READY

1. Find out as much as you can about the test you are going to take. Ask an upperclassman who has had the class (with the same instructor) before; ask the prof in class, if that's possible; visit her in her office if you are still unclear about the form and content of the test. Find out if the exam will be subjective or objective, how long you will have to complete it, what percentage of the final grade it will compose, and what you will need with you when you take it: calculator, blue book, number 2 pencil, scratch paper, etc.

2. Remember that nothing can *replace* thorough knowledge of the material you'll be tested on. You can, however, enhance your chances of showing your instructor how well you have studied and how much you know.

3. Practice recall under all conditions. You know those chemistry formulas frontward and backward when you are sitting at your desk in your room. That's fine; now go to the student lounge and see if you can remember them. Try the library or the cafeteria. You may not have the home field advantage, but at least you won't clutch because the scenery has changed when it

comes time to show what you know.

4. Spread your study time over several days—even weeks—before the exam. If you must cram the night before the exam, go to bed at your regular time and then get up at 3:00 A.M. or 4:00 A.M. to study. You'll be in better shape for the test than if you go to bed at 3:00 A.M. and then try to get up at your regular time.

5. Here's a better idea. Do your heavy studying two nights before the exam. The night before, go to a movie, get a pizza, watch TV—whatever relaxes you. Then get up bright and early, go out for breakfast, jog, get prepared mentally for what's going to happen at test time.

6. Dress up for the test; you'll feel sharper, more confident, better prepared. Make sure, though, that what you wear is comfortable. Don't wear tight jeans that will cut off the circulation in your legs, or a scratchy wool turtleneck sweater that's going to drive you crazy for an hour and fifty-five minutes.

GET SET

1. When you get to class, sit in your regular seat, if you have one. This is not the time to innovate.

2. If you come to class with your head full of data you are on the verge of forgetting, write it on a piece of scratch paper or in the margin of the exam as soon as you are able. Then you can . . .

3. Relax. Chew gum if you need to; do deep breathing; "image" yourself relaxed from head to toe.

4. Listen carefully to all instructions so you understand everything and don't have to ask stupid questions. But *do* ask any legitimate question you have at this point, such as "Can you tell us the relative point value of the questions?" or "May I have another exam? My page 4 didn't duplicate properly."

5. Don't do anything suspicious. Don't put a big box of Junior Mints on your desk; don't ask to go to the restroom during

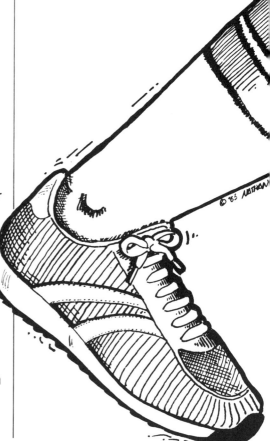

© '83 NATHAN

the test (this requires advance planning); and don't relax by rubbernecking around the room. If the proctor at all suspects that you're cheating, you're done for.

GO!

1. Skim the test. Ask any questions you have at this point such as "Will you please define a word for me?" or "Do you think that there is a numerical typo on question 16?" Determine how much time you will have for each part and spend your time accordingly, keeping in mind the point value of each item.

2. Answer the questions you are absolutely sure about first. Flag those that you didn't answer or that you are unsure of, so you can go back to them later.

3. Don't try to outsmart the test. Just give the information asked for. Generally your first impression of the question is the best one. But if you are confused about what is being asked, get it cleared up with the proctor. If that doesn't help, write a note to the

professor in the margin explaining how you understand the question. Do this only if you think there is a plausible ambiguity that should be addressed.

4. Try to view the test as a whole. The answer to one question may be contained in another question.

5. There are a number of different types of test questions which often require different strategies. Study the question types below for helpful hints in getting through the various parts of a test.

a. Multiple choice questions:

1). Watch out for words like "always," "never" and "all." These usually (not "always") indicate that that particular answer is wrong.

2). Read all the options before marking your answer, even if you think you already have the right choice. There may be a "righter" answer farther down the list.

3). If you must guess, do so only after eliminating the choices you are absolutely sure are wrong.

4). The correct answer is often more general or more specific than the other options.

5). Choices (b), (c) and (d) are more often right than (a) and (e).

6). The answer should match the question grammatically. If it does not, that's a clue that it probably is not correct.

7). Two options may contain a similar sounding word

(elocution and electrocution), or may be identical except for a word or two. If in doubt, choose one of these.

b. True-False questions:

1). Again, watch for mandatory words—"must," "always," "never." These are *usually* false.

2). A statement with the words "normally," "seldom" or "generally" for the most part is trying to tell you the answer is "True."

3). If the statement seems very specific, it is probably true.

4). Don't be confused by double negatives. "Never misunderstood" means "always understood."

c. Fill-in-the-blank and short answer questions:

1). Follow the question's grammar. For example: "Lions are carnivorous, cows are herbivorous and humans are _____." The correct answer is omnivorous. Don't say that humans are omnivores, even though they are. (And don't say they are vegetarians, although that is sometimes true—see #3 above)

2). Look to other questions for answers. If a question reads: "It is _____ to completely control an epidemic," and one of the essay questions is "List six reasons why epidemics are uncontrollable," your answer to the first question is "impossible."

3). Guess if you have to. Don't get too cute, but a parting shot is probably better than no shot at all. (I once got full credit on an anthropology mid-term in October for putting "Happy Halloween" in a short-answer blank. There are some profs who don't go for that sort of thing, though; so watch out.)

d. Essay questions:

1). If you have the option of answering, say, two of four questions, read *all* of them very carefully to make sure you are answering those you know the most about.

2). Take a minute or two to plan what you will write. Jot down your salient points on a piece of scratch paper if you can. Spend at least one paragraph each on an introduction and conclusion which should, by the way, more or less agree with each other. Don't waste time restating the question, even though this might seem like a great way to pad your answer. It won't be appreciated.

3). If you really can't answer a question, don't fake it. It is probably better to compose a relevant and worthwhile question of your own and answer that one, with apologies to your professor. The worst she can do is give you no credit, which is probably what she would do anyway if she knew you were trying to snow her.

4). If you find that you are running out of time and won't be able to answer an essay question (they're almost always at the end of a test), jot the important facts in the space provided before you hand in the test. You will certainly get some credit even though you did not develop your discussion formally.

6. If you are using a computer-graded sheet, check the number on the answer sheet with the test *often* to make sure you aren't off a space. You must not neglect to do this, as one misplaced answer can bolix the whole works.

7. It is invariably better to guess than to leave a question blank.

THE BIG FINISH

1. It is the rare student who is justified in leaving an exam before the allotted time is over. Check and recheck your answers. Correct your spelling and punctuation. Remember, though, that if you took a wild stab at a question which stumped you completely, it's probably better *not* to change such an answer if you start to have second thoughts. Unless some new intelligence jumps into your consciousness, your original hunch is more likely to be right.

2. If as you hand in your test you are 100 percent sure you flubbed, *now* is the time to talk to your professor—not when you see your grade. If she is administering the exam, lay it on her now. Otherwise, hightail it to her office, track her down in the teacher's lounge, whatever. Tell her you did poorly and *why*. (You must have a better excuse than that you didn't study or attend class.) A death in the family, a trashed love affair, or personal illness—if legitimate—are good reasons for doing poorly. If she seems inclined, ask for the opportunity to retake the exam, write a term paper or do an extra-credit project over Christmas vacation. *This advice is only for serious students.* Don't expect to get any sympathy if

Don't-You-Wish-You-Were-That-Quick Department

The proctor had clearly stated that all blue books would be handed in at 11:55 and that any tests received even one minute later would not be considered for grading; late students would have to take an F on the final.

And sure enough, at 11:57 one of the 350 freshman students taking the test came bounding down the steps of the lecture hall with his late exam.

"Sorry. No exams accepted past 11:55. You're out of luck."

"But, I—" began the freshman.

"There are no exceptions."

"Sir, do you know who I am?"

"No, and I don't—"

"Good," said the tardy student and shoved his blue book into the middle of the two-foot-deep pile of exams.

—an old and reportedly true story which if you haven't heard it yet, you soon will, from a kid who knew a kid who was in the class when it happened.

you've been skipping Botany lab all semester and don't have the slightest idea what photo-synthesis is. Remember that you will have to actually *write* that paper or *do* that project, so don't volunteer hastily.

3. When your test is returned to you and you see your grade, get the correct answers for the questions you missed. Class time may be allotted for this or you may need to make an appointment with your instructor. This is especially important on a mid-term test (since you'll be tested on the material again) or if the class is in a field you'll continue to study.

4. A bad score may be a computer error. This happens, and more often than you might suspect (I think it's because they let graduate students do the programming). If you believe you may be the victim of a computer glitch, tell your instructor. If you get no satisfaction go to the registrar and have her look into it.

5. If you think you were graded unfairly or inaccurately be sure you have the proof to back up your claim before you come steaming into the professor's office.

6. Save your test. You can use it later for review.

Unless you go to a super-progressive school, you will find that exams—more than term papers or projects—are the basis on which your entire college experience will be judged. You must learn to take exams well.

There are books in your school library which will go into greater detail on how to study throughout the semester and how to get over test anxiety if that is a problem.

You'll take a lot of tests in college and if you learn right away how to ace them, *the rewards are great!* My brother-in-law is a great test-taker. In high school, he heard one afternoon that there was going to be a Betty Crocker Homemaker contest after school, and the winner would get a $200 scholarship. The basis for winning was a test. He took the test that afternoon and finished second, not knowing a thing about cooking or Home Ec. He tested out of most of his freshman and sophomore courses in college. After graduation, he was one of the few people probably ever to take all ten CPA exams at once and pass them all the first time around.

Yes, he's smarter than your average bear, but it shows up on paper because he knows how to take a test. The time you spend honing your skills will be well worth it. Good luck!

TERM PAPER FINESSE

Whatever you call them—essays, reports, themes, compositions, dissertations—they are the bane of all students, and they'll follow you through your college days like a curse. That being the case, it only makes sense to learn the finer points of term paper finesse. Here are five tips that will help you get your term papers favorably noticed.

Get a Good Book

There are scores of books in the library and in the college bookstore with titles like *How to Write a Term Paper* or *Better Term Papers in 10 Easy Lessons.* Get your hands on one of these, study it, and follow its advice. It will help enormously.

It would also be a good idea to get a book on style. There are several accepted style books, and they are invaluable for all matters regarding the written word. Where else are you going to find out whether to use a semicolon or a comma, how to properly construct footnotes, the subtle habits of hyphens, who and what should be capitalized and when—in short, all those details you never wonder about until you're three pages into a term paper that's due in four hours and it's five o'clock in the morning.

Some colleges adopt one book as the last word for every paper written in that college. When this is the case, there will be an ample supply of the books in the college bookstore. Get one and follow it to the letter; once informed, you'll have no excuse for not doing so.

Get It Typed

When your instructor says all term papers must be typed he's talking about *yours*. But it doesn't necessarily follow that you have to be the one to type it. If typing for you is an exercise in despair, get someone else to do it for you. It will cost a little but there's no sense in being a masochist about this. There are professional typists who will be glad to help—they're easy to find. Some will even pick up and deliver and correct minor spelling and grammatical errors to boot. The mental health you preserve will be fair compensation for the cost, and you can find more constructive ways to use your time—like studying or getting a part-time job to pay the typist.

If you are working on a computer, make sure your printer gives you letter-quality printing, or close to it.

You must *never* under-estimate the importance of a clean, well-typed manuscript! It is essential to a good grade. Fresh, crisp, sparkling copy will get your paper noticed if for no other reason than it says to your instructor that you cared enough to give your best. That means using a fresh ribbon—or carbon ribbon, better still—on good quality bond paper—no flimsy cheap stuff or that horrid "erasable" junk.

Remember, by the time the instructor reaches for your term paper he will have graded dozens of other papers. He will be tired and looking for any excuse not to read it. Don't give him any. Dirty, dog-eared, smudged, erased, and struck-over copy is an invitation to ditch your paper and scribble a "C" in the gradebook. Neatness counts big with professors because so few students take the time to do it right. Make sure you're one of the few who do.

Get a Cover

Once you've got the thing neatly—that is, *perfectly*—typed, put on the finishing touch with a cover. This is a small expense and well worth it.

A cover tells the instructor that you took the assignment seriously, that you respect your work and that he should too.

Don't get fancy, though. The rule is quiet elegance. Binding your term paper with colored yarn and writing the title page in blue glitter will not cut it in college. The way to get your paper noticed is not through derision and ridicule, which you will certainly earn if you produce anything bizarre. Paperclips and staples are out, too. They make term papers too hard to handle; the clips fall off and scatter the pages while staples snag on everything. You don't want an F because your paper snagged the instructor's favorite alpaca sweater. Play it safe and get the kind of cover that can be removed easily by the instructor so that he can have complete access to your scintillating prose. These covers can also be recycled.

Get a Little Personal

It is often a good idea to clip a brief note to the title page or cover. In it you can say anything you believe will get the professor in the right frame of mind to read your paper and explain anything that might be misunderstood, thus:

> Professor Fist: I enjoyed doing the research for this paper on the effect of the Puritan work ethic on unionization in the '30s. You will notice a slight digression on the subject of John L. Lewis's childhood. I was able to get a personal interview with his dentist's granddaughter, who informed me that his father was a minister in the Reformed church. The ramifications of their relationship intrigued me to the point that . . .

Keep it short, and don't get too sappy or apologetic. Include a note of this kind *only* if you think it will improve your grade.

"There is something fascinating about science. One gets such wholesale returns of conjecture out of such trifling investments of fact."

Mark Twain

Get It in on Time

The one way you *don't* want your paper distinguished is by its tardiness. A late paper automatically drops in value as the deadline recedes. If for any reason you think you might miss the deadline, talk to your instructor well in advance of the due date. Who knows? With a valid excuse you might earn yourself an extension, which you certainly won't by meandering into class and announcing casually, "My paper's not ready yet." Timeliness is next to godliness where term papers are concerned.

SUNDAY NIGHT SUGGESTIONS FOR MONDAY MORNING TERM PAPER

Stuck for a topic? Try one of these:

—Beetlemania: A Psycho-history of the Work of Insect Psychiatrist John-Paul Georgianringo

—Primitive Doubleknit Weavers of the Pitcairn Islands: New Proof for the Leisure Suits of the Gods

—Little, White, Dirty and Barefaced: A Compendium of Political Lies

—The Future of Ivory Soap in the Decline of Elephant Populations

—Sunburn: A Hot New Source of Solar Energy

—A Nation of Millionaires: What Inflation Is Doing to America

—Pneumoultramicrosopicsilicovocanoconiosis: Is the Disease Actually Worse Than the Spelling?

—Why Johnny Can't Spell: Commun Spelling Errers Amung Freshmen

—The Role of Classical Music in the Making of Cultured Pearls

—North Dakota: Fact or Fiction?

—Death and Taxes: Is There a Cure?

—Growing up Normal: A Personal Case History

—Zero Base Financing for Students with Zero Finances

—Pac Mac: The New Video-Food Craze

—Heaven Can Wait: A Study of Religious Procrastination

—Television: Is It Here to Stay?

—King Kong: The Complete History of American Royalty

—Making Ends Meat: The Use of Fillers in the Hot Dog Industry

NEVER SAY "D," or HOW TO GET A GRADE CHANGED

1. No grade is final. If you think you got one you don't deserve, or one that you can't live with, do not hesitate to try to get it changed.

2. Errors of computation are not unheard of. Some of the more common ones:

—you made an error in using the computer score sheet when you took a test.

—the computer's program for grading your test was faulty.

—the test-grader added up your right answers incorrectly.

—at the end of the term the professor figured your

average incorrectly.

—you handed in a paper or test or project without your name on it, so a 0 was recorded.

—your lab project was not credited to your grade.

—your attendance in class was not recorded.

—there was a mix-up when the grade was entered by the registrar.

If you believe that one of these has occurred, take your proof to your professor and ask for a review of your grade.

3. You may have a disagreement with your professor as to the right answer on a test question or the validity of your research work or term paper thesis. Make an appointment with him and be prepared to argue your point. If you are successful in convincing him you may receive additional credit.

4. There may be extenuating circumstances which caused you to perform uncharacteristically. Perhaps there was a death in your family or you had personal illness or an emotional trauma which made it difficult or impossible for you to do well on a test or complete a paper on time. Make an appointment with your professor and explain the situation to her. Most professors are sympathetic to personal crises and will be open to reviewing a poor grade under such conditions.

5. If the poor grade you received was pretty much your fault, you may suggest remedial work that could raise your marks. For example, you might volunteer to do an extra-credit project or help out with the professor's lab project over the holiday or retake the test. If you come to your professor with a reasonable plan you may get a second chance. Remember, though, that you will actually have to *do* the work you promised, so don't get too carried away.

6. Do not lie, do not cry. And do not make your professor feel like a dolt for his addition error or failure to see that he misworded the essay question. Do not overstate your case or expect unmerited consideration. Be sincere and willing to accept the outcome of your plea. If you are absolutely convinced that you received a raw deal, and your instructor is totally unsympathetic you can appeal the grade to an academic review committee. Check your college handbook for procedural details.

FAKING IT: THE ART OF
OBFUSCATION

In those tenuous moments when an excuse or an explanation is necessary—for that late paper, that missed appointment, that forgotten assignment—a masterful application of the fine art of obfuscation could save the day. They can't yell at you quite so loud if they don't know what you're talking about. What is more, if you're convincing, you might even win a second chance. Here's what we mean:

Don't say: *Instead, say:*

"I forgot."

"Phrenialogically speaking, the aforementioned subject ineluctably eluded my short-term mnemonic functions, resulting in an unaccountable cognition void."

"It'll be a little late."

"Indefeasible difficulties necessitate a reassessment of allotted time parameters vis a vis the restructuring of predesignated completion goals."

"My dog ate it."

"The ordinarily carnivorous domestic canine under my husbandry purloined unprecedented masticatory privileges with my unobserved project."

"I lost it."

"Indivertible circumstances misdirected the successful ensconcement of the errant property rendering possessorship inoperative."

"I overslept."

"Due to an avouched preponderancy for somnolent indulgence, I unilaterally misapprehended the foreordained commencement of this scholastic exercise."

"It isn't finished."

"The effectual consumation of the assignated object was inexplicably prolonged by irremediable forces unresponsive to my personal influence."

"I flunked."	"The variable achievement gradient assiduously ascribed a regrettably unpropitious exponential symbol to the diagnostic instrument which I benignly submitted for judicious academic consideratory purposes."
"I broke it."	"Owing to the delicate quiddity of the foredoomed article, my innoxious scrutiny stressed certain heretofore undisclosed flaws in manufacture, precipitating an inevitable fracture of the maldesigned subcomponents."
"I didn't study."	"The overwhelmingly addictive character of televised divertissements short-circuited my ambitionary regard for the apprehension and retention of the opusculatory material now under consideration."
"My dad won't let me."	"My paternal guardian whimsically elected to curtail his offspring's natural inclination toward inoffensive tenebrious perambulation of a salubrious nature."
"I wrecked the car."	"Despite my keen affiliation with Newtonian physics of motion, pernicious forces beyond my control superintervened, wreaking havoc with the forward momentum of the internal combustion vehicle conscribed to my care, thereby necessitating minor restructuring of the more malleable automotive protuberances."
"I don't want to go out with you."	"Attractive as is the immanent prospect of an amorous interlude, and not unsympathetic to the solicitous encouchment of your request, I nevertheless deem it emotionally incumbent to more realistically confine my courtship practices to members of the immediate human species."
"I fell asleep in class."	"Notwithstanding the scintillating repartage concommitant to this scholastic assemblage, intransigent preternatural biologic functions conspired to surmount my fragile resolve, plunging consciousness beneath my direct autonomy and thus insuring a rapid decline into somnolency."

Practicalities 6

"Never put off till tomorrow what you can do the day after tomorrow."

Mark Twain

MINUTE BY MINUTE

A CRASH COURSE IN TIME MANAGEMENT

Make a list. Nurture the habit of list-making—everything you have to do for the day should be on the list, prioritized in order of importance. Do first things first.

Break large tasks into smaller ones. This keeps the megajobs from overwhelming you by sheer magnitude. Instead of writing "research term paper" on your list, you should put "go to the library," "check out card catalog," "check out *Reader's Guide.*" By breaking one big task into several smaller ones you help insure success.

Work on one thing at a time. Doing one task start to finish gives you momentum as you move through the day. It keeps your energies focused and your mind unburdened with extraneous

matters. The result is that you work more quickly and get more done.

Define all tasks specifically. Your list should contain only precise descriptions of what you want to accomplish. Avoid vague references such as "study history." Instead, put "read Chapter 4 in History text." The more concretely defined, the easier it is to accomplish and the easier to recognize when you have finished.

Set aside a place to work. Make yourself a special work area that has all the things you need for the tasks you have to do. Keep this work nook clean and uncluttered, organized for work and *only* work. When in your work place do work and *only* work. Soon you will feel a sense of accomplishment just by

sitting down in your work chair. You'll work faster and more efficiently in this place because it has what you need and because it has pleasant associations with past performance.

Keep the number of tasks down to a manageable size. Make each day's list one you can complete. If the thing can truly be done tomorrow put it on tomorrow's list. With too big a list you'll feel beaten before you even begin. You want to be able to savor the sweet victory of having reached your goal for the day. If you constantly have leftover tasks spilling into the next day you'll get discouraged as you fall further and further behind.

Check your progress often. Throughout the day refer to your list to see how you're doing. Adjust your speed accordingly. This allows you to give yourself minibreaks throughout the day as you tick things off your list. You can also alternate the hard tasks with easier ones to avoid getting burned out. By knowing where you are at all times you keep from feeling rushed.

Reward yourself. When you have finished your tasks for the day reward yourself. Celebrate your achievement. Take yourself out for a Coke, watch a favorite TV show or treat yourself to a movie or a phone call home—anything that says "job well done." The reward waiting at the end of the list will spur you to heroic heights of industry and keep you from feeling like a drudge.

HOUR AFTER HOUR:

LIVING WITH A STUDY SCHEDULE

We know you hate the thought of a study schedule. You don't think it has value and question the advisability of committing yourself to something that can only make you miserable.

But it really is important for you to get a grasp of when your classes are, when you work, and when you are going to find time to study, have some fun and get some sleep. At the beginning of each quarter or semester you should sit down for a half hour or so and put together a schedule. You don't have to be ruled by it for the next eighteen weeks but if you follow it for at least one week you'll have a better handle on where your time is going. Here is a form you can use:

	MON	TUE	WED	THU	FRI	SAT	SUN
7:00							
8:00							
9:00							
10:00							
11:00							
12:00							
1:00							
2:00							
3:00							
4:00							
5:00							
6:00							
7:00							
8:00							
9:00							
10:00							

First, fill in your classes and labs, thus:

	MON	TUE	WED	THU	FRI	SAT	SUN
7:00	Chem		Chem		Chem		
8:00							
9:00	Calc	Calc	Calc	Calc	Calc		
10:00							
11:00							
12:00							
1:00				Chem Lab			
2:00							
3:00							
4:00		Bowling		Bowling			
5:00							
6:00							
7:00		Art Hist					
8:00							
9:00							
10:00							

Not bad. You also work fifteen hours a week at food service. That needs to be blocked in, along with other commitments: church on Sunday, and Science Club on Wednesday nights, for example.

	MON	TUE	WED	THU	FRI	SAT	SUN
7:00	Chem		Chem		Chem		
8:00							
9:00	Calc	Calc	Calc	Calc	Calc		Church
10:00							
11:00	Work	Work	Work		Work	Work	
12:00							
1:00				Chem Lab			
2:00							
3:00							
4:00		Bowling		Bowling			
5:00							
6:00							
7:00		Art Hist	SciClub				
8:00							
9:00							
10:00							

All the blocks that are not filled in yet represent discretionary time. You need to eat, of course, and you must study. Keep in mind that the guys in the dorm normally have a football or baseball game on Saturday afternoons, and you want to leave weekend nights open for dates and such, and you don't want to count on having to study Sunday afternoon and evening, but you can if you must. So now your schedule looks like this:

	MON	TUE	WED	THU	FRI	SAT	SUN
7:00	Chem	B'fast	Chem	B'fast	Chem	B'fast	
8:00	B'fast	Study	B'fast	Study	B'fast		
9:00	Calc	Calc	Calc	Calc	Calc	Study	Church
10:00							
11:00	Work	Work	Work	Study	Work	Work	
12:00							
1:00				ChemLab			
2:00							
3:00	Study	Study	Study				
4:00		Bowling		Bowling			
5:00							
6:00	Supper	Supper	Supper	Supper			
7:00		ArtHist	SciClub				
8:00	Study		Study				
9:00							
10:00							

You have twenty-five hours of planned study time (probably enough to cover your twelve-hour course load, considering that you have left all day Sunday in reserve), you have your Friday and Saturday nights free, with no studying Friday afternoon (you hardly ever feel like doing it then) and just a few hours with the books on Saturday morning. You are free to hang out at the student union from 10:00 to 11:00 most mornings, and you can bowl an extra game after P.E. class on Tuesdays and Thursdays.

It wouldn't hurt to try planning your activities in this way—and it might work. If you are having trouble with your schedule, then see if you can revise it so it's more workable. And don't be afraid to miss a beat in your day-to-day rhythm. As long as you know where your time is going for the most part you won't be unmade by an occasional digression.

THE DESKTOP LIBRARY

Building your own library is one of the chief (highly underrated) pleasures of life. The best time you'll ever have to begin is in your college years when your exposure and contact with books of all kinds is greater than at any other time of your life.

Beyond that, however, every serious student should have her own library of reference books necessary for her education. But where to begin?

Bible. For a Christian the Bible is, of course, indispensable. For anyone else, this book is important for the reason that most of the world's great thinkers found in it a wellspring of inspiration and challenge. To understand them and their ideas, to understand this country's heritage, to discover the source of all those allusions from Shakespeare, this book is a must.

Dictionary. Any dictionary will *not* do. The thin little paperback they give away at the bank, for example, is not what a student needs. Get a dictionary that 1) has enough words: somewhere around 100,000 is adequate; 2) is current: updated within the last five years; 3) is easy to read: well-printed on good paper with understandable explanations. *Webster's Collegiate Dictionary* is excellent on all counts.

Thesaurus. Not a duck-billed denizen of the Mesozoic, this is the treasury of all wordsmiths. The thesaurus collects words and sorts them out into groupings according to ideas. Need another word for "sad"? The thesaurus has dozens. The dictionary form is easiest to use but a larger thesaurus is more informative and helpful once you learn how to use it. *Roget's University Thesaurus* is a good pick.

Atlas. Even though you're not a Geography major (who is?), you'll still need to know where things are happening around the world. How else are you going to find out

Afganistan's total area in square miles (250,775)? Or the distance between Amsterdam and Bangkok (5,707 miles)? Or, where Mohammedanism is popular (all over the place)? Rand McNally makes a good atlas, and there are others. Stay away from picture atlases—not enough hard information.

Book of quotations.

There's nothing like a provocative quotation or two or a snappy aphorism to spice up a term paper or essay. The library has dozens of these books; trouble is, the library is closed at 2 A.M. when you're laying on the finishing touches and need that quote the most. You should have a book of quotations of your own; they come in all sizes and some are even slanted toward specific areas, such as the humanities or arts.

Book of style. No, not the

fall fashion issue of *Seventeen.* We're talking writing style here. It might surprise you to learn that there are different, yet equally acceptable ways to write footnotes and punctuate sentences, among other things. It's called style and there are several arbiters you should be aware of. The main one, naturally, is the one your school ascribes to. Your English prof can tell you which book the school favors, if any. *The Chicago Manual of Style* is a favorite among many. If your school has no preference, you could not go wrong with *The Washington Post Deskbook on Style.* It's easy to read and understand and it's easy to look

things up fast. Don't sit there and *guess* whether to use lie, lay or laid or whether to spell out one hundred thousand, or write 100,000—look it up!

Writing form book. In

addition to a general book of style, you would do well to include in your personal library a book which is aimed specifically at college and graduate students who are writing term papers and theses. Here are some excellent ones:

MLA Handbook for Writers of Research Papers, Theses, and Dissertations, by Joseph Gibaldi, 4th edition, The Modern Language Association of America, New York, 1995 (updated periodically).

Form and Style: Theses, Reports, Term Papers, by William G. Campbell, Stephen V. Ballou, and Carole Slade, Houghton-Mifflin, Boston, 1982.

The Craft of Research, by W.C. Booth, G.C. Colomb and J.M. Williams, University of Chicago Press, 1995.

A Manual for Writers of Term Papers, Theses, and Dissertations, by Kate L. Turabian, 6th edition, University of Chicago Press, 1996.

Books such as these usually begin with a guide to choosing a topic. The meat of what they have to say is on how to footnote, how to do the bibliography, what is plagiarism and what isn't, and how to determine margins and spacing when you type the paper.

COMPUTERS GO TO COLLEGE

All you need is a 10MHz IBM-compatible microprocessor with at least 640K RAM and two 360K floppies to back-up a 40 megabyte hard disk, six expansion slots, two serial ports, a multimode video adapter, an expanded keyboard configured with an optical mouse, internal modem, graphics card, game port, and an 18-pin dot matrix, or 720 dpi laser printer, and you're flying, Jack.

Did you understand any of that? If you did, read no further. This chapter is not for you.

If, however, you are one of the millions whose eyes glaze over at the mere mention of modems and megabytes, relax. Don't panic. It is not necessary to own a computer in order to succeed in college.

School is still mostly concerned with dozing through lectures, scribbling notes, sleeping in the library, and sucking down Cokes in the Student Union—tasks that have not yet been fully adapted to the computer age. Computers don't take exams, and they don't earn degrees. They won't even show up for your 7:30 Chem Lab when you oversleep.

Networking at Your College

How do computers fit in on *your* campus? This is a key question and easy to answer. Find out what your college computing center recommends and what is provided in terms of networking, hook-ups in the residence halls, and deals on hardware and software.

Do PCs (i.e., IBM-compatibles) or Macintoshes tend to dominate? In other words, what sort of technical support, networking, compatible hardware among your friends and experts in the dorms will you find? Will a desktop or a laptop suit your needs better? One college recently began issuing laptops to freshman to use during their four years on campus.

Will you be given an e-mail account? Is there an extra charge for that? What access will you have to the World Wide Web? One very positive fact is that universities have long been connected electronically, long before those "www" addresses started popping up on TV commercials and ads in periodicals.

Pluses and Minuses

The biggest argument against computers is spelled m-o-n-e-y with a capital $. A good, basic machine with a printer and the programs you'll need to run it (not to mention printer cartridges, paper, disks, and such) will set you back a thousand, at least. Of course, if you insist on spending, the sky is the limit: modems, laser printers, color monitors, CD-ROM drives, laptops, etc. The cost can quickly run to tens of thousands.

Then there is the learning curve to consider. Unless you are prepared to master the technical jargon (see above) you will likely find living with a computer more of a cold war than peaceful co-existence. And becoming competent also requires an enormous time investment.

Suppose you invest in a computer today. Will it be the computer you want or need in a year or three? Probably not. Talk about programmed obsolescence, computers come and go faster than fashion trends—and that's saying something.

Ask yourself: "Do I really need it?" Usually, the answer will be: "It depends." What do you want to do with the computer? Or, put another way, what do you want the computer to do for you?

For example, your PC can bang out that fourth draft of your term paper like nobody's business. Word processing—shoving words around on screen and then printing them on paper, flawlessly, time after time—is one of the things computers do best. It's called applications in computer jargon, and some of these *applications* are excellent.

The enormous expense of computers, listed as a liability above, can become less so through intelligent shopping. There *is* low-cost equipment out there, but you have to know where to look—not in the Yellow Pages, but in want-ads and on the campus bulletin boards.

Because of the volatility of the computer marketplace (obsolescence, remember?), used computers have very low resale value. Watch the want-ads and you can pick up a very good deal on the machine you want second-hand (often right out of the box, from someone who didn't have quite the "need" for the machine that he thought he did). Looking through the want-ads also has the advantage of free software, since most people tend to sell out lock, stock, and barrel, and will include the expensive programs with the computer.

Many people are leery of electronics bought second-hand, and think that new is the only way to go. But computers aren't like cars. As one expert told me, "Either they work out of the box, or they don't. If they do, they'll probably work forever." With electronics, internal problems are usually discovered in the first few hours of use. This means you don't have quite the worry when buying second-hand; if the first owner didn't have any problems, chances are you won't either. In any event, ask for a 10-day bring-it-back guarantee to cover any unforeseen gliches.

One Final Thought

If you're thinking a computer would be handy, but can't quite swing the finances, or aren't sure whether you want to devote the time and energy to mastering a second language, maybe you won't need to. Many colleges and universities now provide computer labs the way they used to provide typing rooms. The purpose is the same: help students get their written work in readable form.

Usually, you bring your own data disk and plug into any available machine—often, programs are also provided. Printers are available for whacking out your deathless prose.

So, it could well be your investment in the computer age need only run to a box of diskettes, some paper, and a program or two. Later on, if you find you require a better working arrangement than the school's catch-as-catch-can operation, often with interminable lines at the end of the term, you'll know what you need, and what the machine can do for you.

Then again, you might want to wait until they come up with a computer that will not only wake you for class, but will screen your messages, serve nutritious meals, and supply you with hot coffee during finals week. Hold it, they already did: it's called Mom.

The Well-Stocked Desk

College is not all reading, discussing and drinking coffee. Consider the following items, most of which can be had for better prices at office discount stores than at the campus bookstore.

Address book
Backpack
Bookends
Bulletin board
Calculator
Computer disks
Correction fluid
Desk lamp
File box (for hanging files
    and folders)
Glue
Highlighter pens
Key chain
Paper (spiral notebooks or
    loose-leaf)

Paper clips
Pencil sharpener
Pens and pencils
Rubber bands
Ruler
Scissors
Stamps
Stapler
Stationery
Student planner calendar
Tape (adhesive and masking)
Thumbtacks

After Hours 7

SIDELINES

"Look, I barely have time to show up at class and do all the studying I'll have to do to keep my 3.5. I don't have time to attend some dumb Thespians meeting every week. I can't imagine it'll do me any good."

"You guys go on without me. No, really, I gotta hit the books this afternoon. Hey, Jim Barker down the hall is a tall guy—ask *him* if he wants to play volleyball."

"Sure I'm for Dale Summers, but I don't have time to do any of that campaigning stuff with you. I don't know how they expect students to do much good anyway, and the campaign is the same time as mid-terms. I just can't risk committing myself to the campaign and then coming up short on study time. Sorry."

Are extracurricular activities important? Sure they are! But for every goof-off who can't *ever* think of anything more important to do than play Frisbee golf when he should be in class, there is the student who is afraid to get involved in anything that won't put a grade on the transcript.

Why? Maybe it's the feeling that doing well in the classroom is the *only* valid goal for a student—any activity which might possibly detract from it is to be avoided. Some students must carry such a heavy class and workload that they genuinely have little time to do anything else, much as they would like to. Others like to come and go as they please and don't want to commit themselves to something that might curtail their freedom. Even though there are defensible reasons for confining oneself to class attendance and study, there are also good reasons to branch out a bit and pursue other activities:

1. **You deserve a break. All work and no play makes Jack a dull boy. Easy does it.** You'll do better in school if you make sure that some time is spent relaxing, playing, socializing. The strain of study is great and an occasional break will be good for you. When you go back to your desk you'll be clearheaded, refreshed and ready to hit the books with renewed energy.

You'll also do better in life if you recognize that play and recreation are important components of successful living. The scholar in his ivory tower and the workaholic executive are both pitiable examples of people who have misjudged the importance of work. *Nothing is worth anything until it touches another person,* and that goes for all the facts and figures and places and dates you will be expected to learn during your college career. *Now* is the time to develop habits you will practice for the rest of your life. Give relationships and recreation a place of honor on your list of values.

2. **Extracurricular activities are part of the education you came to college to get.** It's good for a Sociology major to do some volunteer work with illiterate adults in the inner city; for a Biology major to take a long walk in the woods during spring; for a PoliSci major to attend a town meeting. Balancing classroom study with practical experiences enables you to see the end result of what you are learning.

If it is not impossible, it is at least difficult to understand the full ramifications of what is being taught in the classroom without viewing its application in the field. Most schools try their best to provide this marriage for their students through labs, field trips, internships. But the responsibility for reconciling theory to practice may rest on your shoulders entirely. Finding a place to work with newly-learned skills and apply newly-acquired knowledge will bring you in touch with reality and help you make judgments about your decisions. Many people are unhappy now in the jobs they prepared for in college because they didn't know what

they were getting into before it was too late. Don't be one of those! Find out where you're headed *now.*

3. **Your future employer will ask you about it.** If you are being considered for a position with a company they will want to know if you are the kind of person who will be content to merely do the 9-to-5 routine or if you will be a self-starter, a motivated learner, a go-the-extra-miler. But you won't be asked if you are all those wonderful things; more likely you'll be asked, "Did you belong to any public-service clubs in college?" "Were you active in your church?" "Have you been elected to any club or school office?" If you are able to answer "yes" to these kinds of questions you will communicate that you don't do only what is required—you do more.

Some universities have developed a mentoring-transcript program, which is an opportunity to get your nonclassroom achievements and experiences verified by the staff or faculty of the university and filed with the registrar so that people who read your transcript get not only your GPA but an idea of what else you learned in college. This innovation is further proof that it *is* important to expand the concept of what constitutes a learning experience to include outings with friends, volunteer work, club membership, intramural sports events, dating, church involvement and other extracurricular activities.

IN TRANSIT

Mustang Sally

The first thing that comes to mind when thinking of campus transportation is a car of your own. But contrary to what *The American Way of Life Rulebook* teaches, you do not need an automobile to make it big in college. In fact, a car can be a big nuisance on campus and cause you a lot of trouble.

For one thing, there's the cost. Unless you own your limo free and clear, you undoubtedly have

monthly payments to make. Then there's upkeep. And repairs, which come when you least expect and can ill afford them. Don't forget gasoline, insurance—which is astronomically high for students—and the vehicle license, which can run into hundreds of dollars a year depending on the type of car you have and where you live.

Then add on top of all this the fact that the administration doesn't *want* students to have cars, and goes out of its way to discourage them. They assess parking fees somewhere in the neighborhood of two years' tuition, not to mention speed bumps every fifty feet on the main access roads and parking lots which may be no nearer than .75 miles from any academic building or residence hall.

Still, there is a certain prestige that goes with owning your own car. You'll be the envy of every other student who must rely solely on footpower to get where he's going. But since most kids won't have their own set of wheels, you'll end up lending yours to friends, friends of friends and friends of friends of friends. Decide ahead of time if that's the way you want to gain popularity.

If you live off campus, owning a car may be a near necessity for you—regardless of any drawbacks. Your work schedule or extracurricular activities may also make it imperative that you have your private coach to use whenever you need it. To own or not to own is a judgment call that you must make based on the campus you're on, your financial resources and your special needs.

Commuters should make every attempt to carpool with other students—teachers even. Don't overlook the profs as a prime source of transportation to and from classes. They'll have a schedule similar to yours and the same days off; they live off campus; they're not so rich that they couldn't use some help with commuting expenses; they're likely to have a fairly adequate automobile.

Resident students, too, can share a car. You might arrange with your roommate to let her use your buggy on a regular basis to get to her job in exchange for a tank of gas a week or charge her so-much-per-mile for its use. Of course if you have a brother or sister who is on campus too, that's an excellent opportunity to pitch in together to absorb the cost of a car.

Two Wheels Are Better Than None

Motorcycles, mopeds and bicycles are perhaps the most efficient means of private transportation for students. Two-wheelers are initially less expensive than a car; the operating costs are lower and repairs don't cost an arm and a leg. They also give you greater parking flexibility. You can ride your Schwinn right up to your destination and chain it to the rack provided or a convenient post. When you get back to the dorm or apartment, you can take it inside with you where it will be safe and protected from the elements. Even motorcycles and mopeds can be parked in places where cars aren't allowed.

Disadvantages? 1) Usefulness may be curtailed by terrain and/or disagreeable weather. If you're attending the University of Alaska you might want to leave your Yamaha at home. 2) There are fewer ancillary uses than a car (i.e., no good at a drive-in movie, generally unsuitable for formal events, limited hauling capacity).

Another One Rides the Bus

Nearly every community is endowed with some form of public transportation. It may be a city bus line, commuter train, elevated train, subway or taxi service (add cable cars for San Francisco residents). Public transportation is generally reliable in its own way; the bus may be a few minutes late getting to your stop, but if it needs a brake job they'll put another vehicle in service so that you *can* get to school. Even commuters who pay up to $1.00 for a fare find that, as high as that seems, it is usually cheaper than owning a car.

While any public conveyance you use runs on *its* schedule—not yours—there is a welcome independence in being able to catch the bus or train whenever you want. Once you've learned the various routes, transfer points, procedures and timetables you'll value your freedom from the fallibility of automobiles, the whimsy of the weather and the lack of punctuality on the part of your peers.

Problems

Regardless of the type of transportation you have or do not have, you should look into your alternatives should an unexpected situation arise. Especially if you are a commuting student, have "Plan B" and "Plan C" in reserve at all times.

If you are in a car pool, get the class and work schedule of all involved (including applicable phone numbers), so you know who to turn to in case the designated driver can't make it; find out if a person who normally doesn't drive can *ever* get hold of a vehicle. Know about other car pools which might be available on an emergency basis. Know what buses and trains could be used if you get in a jam, and know how long it would take you to walk (or run!) to class if you had to.

Before you need one, ask around about good mechanics, reputable garages in town and bicycle repair shops. Search out kids on campus who can do a tune-up or a brake adjustment and other minor work. Especially if you have a foreign or older car, you will have difficulty getting reliable repairs on the spur of the moment; parts will be hard to get and you might get cheated if you allow yourself to be at the mercy of the first guy who promises to put your chariot back in working condition.

Trains and Boats and Planes

The really big trip is going to be the one you take to school in the fall, home on weekends and holidays and back home again in the summer.

Ride-sharing is the most time-honored tradition when it comes to getting back and forth (not hitchhiking, which we do not recommend at all). If you're already at school watch the bulletin boards for notices or post one yourself.

You can write to the college ahead of time—during the summer—and they will tell you of other students who live in your home town or general vicinity. Then you can make arrangements on your own.

Car rental agencies sometimes hire people to drive their cars from one place to another when they have too many vehicles in a city that doesn't need them. Actually, they don't hire as much as they let a person drive the car, reimbursing for gas and oil. This is often a great way to get a really nice car for nothing. To explore possibilities, check the classifieds or call the local auto leasing companies in your area.

Bus lines, trains and airline companies are usually a more expensive means of transport (although some kids could fly first class for what they pay in parking tickets alone). You can keep the cost down by investigating competitive rates and taking advantage of promotions such as two-for-one fares, Super-Savers or standby rates. A travel agent will be helpful in getting the best deal. Don't worry about it costing extra—it doesn't; the airlines and bus lines and train companies pay the agent.

A word of warning: some popular runs should be avoided at peak times. For example, there is a train that goes between Carbondale, Illinois and Chicago that is a zoo—an outright, animal-toting zoo—when all the big city kids who are attending U of I want to get home for Christmas vacation. More tickets are sold than seats available. Apparently some kids don't mind sleeping in the overhead luggage racks and sitting on their suitcases in the aisle, but you might. So ask around about the travel conditions *before* you catch the first bus or train after finals are over.

Bon voyage!

Shipping Your Bicycle

Train: Your assembled bike can go right along with you—in the baggage car. You will be charged just a few extra dollars when you travel tandem; if you put the bike on the train by itself, you'll pay according to weight and size and how far it's going.

Plane: The bike must be broken down—at least the handlebars and pedals must come off. Usually the airline will provide a container or box which it can be placed in. Rates vary. Check different charges made by different airlines.

Bus: The bike may travel free with you if it's no larger than 24″ x 24″ x 45″. Without you, the cost will depend upon the weight of the bike (size requirement is the same) and the distance it's going.

Plan ahead: Save the box your bike came in, and use that for transporting it later. If you threw the box away, check with a bike shop to see if they have any.

GOING GREEK

After a decade or more of decline in participation—due largely to student activism and antiestablishmentarianism (hey, we finally found a way to use that word in a sentence!)—fraternities and sororities on college campuses are experiencing a revival. It is once again important to college students to pledge into the "right" house as a freshman, to participate in the Greek system.

Many colleges, especially Christian colleges, forbid fraternities and sororities; other schools, junior colleges for example, have none because their type of school or campus does not lend itself to the system.*

Pledging *is* important, but not so much because one sorority or fraternity is more desirable than another. It is important because each student who decides to go through "hell week" should be aware that membership in *any* fraternity or sorority is an issue under debate.

Supporters of the Greek system say that membership helps the student find a niche in the college community; provides a social network; creates a structure through which community and campus problems can be addressed; encourages students to do well academically (by means of grade point average minimums which must be maintained by members).

That sounds fine. What's the problem?

The problems are many.

1. Students are invited to join a fraternity or sorority. Very often the invitation is based on such dubious applicant qualifications as personal appearance, athletic ability, wealth or family ties to the chapter (the old boy network). Members of racial and religious minorities have traditionally been excluded from membership; in response, some have formed their own chapters.

2. Most fraternities and sororities practice "hazing," which is an initiation regimen for pledges (those

who wish to join). Every year, a few students are accidentally killed during hazing and more are seriously injured. Some upperclassman fraternity brothers still think that they should test the mettle of pledges in some stupid and outlandish way—such as forcing them to drink two fifths of gin and then swim across an icy-cold campus creek. Some psychologists say that hazing strengthens the inductee's loyalty to the group. Maybe. But is the price worth it?

3. While most fraternities and sororities present themselves to the community as civic-minded organizations, the majority of their activities are likely to revolve around drinking. This is especially true of fraternities. Perhaps more than anything else, it has been this preoccupation with recreational drinking among young people who are often not of legal age or developmental maturity to do so responsibly that has given the Greek system a bad name.

4. Sorority or fraternity membership involves a slavish commitment to conformity. Sorority pledges have been known to receive instruction in how to flick the ashes off a cigarette (you are to roll the lit end in the ashtray, for those of you who are curious), how to dress, what boys are suitable to date (invariably boys who belong to fraternities—often to one specific fraternity) and how to carry school books. One can often tell what fraternity or sorority a student belongs to by a characteristic hair or clothing style or manner of speech that the group has adopted.

Perhaps it is unfair to make broad negative statements about fraternities and sororities. From campus to campus their nature varies somewhat. Some are open to virtually anyone who wishes to join and it may not necessarily be expensive or difficult to do so. On other campuses the competition between houses is cutthroat and the whole system provides very little to recommend itself to concerned, intelligent students.

Many Christian kids join sororities and fraternities. They are able to maintain their own personal standards of conduct within such a group, and are a positive influence on other members. They argue—convincingly—that it is important for Christians to be present and visible in every facet of society, in every group on a college campus. They see no serious conflict between their Christian principles and the goals and practices of the group.

You are the only one who can decide for you. Your decision to be involved in the Greek system—or to reject it—should be based on more than unexamined feelings and social pressures. Instead, make an informed decision. Find out what you are getting into and consider the statement that will be made by your actions.

---

*There are scholastic fraternities which are open to students who excel in various areas, such as music or chemistry; anyone who meets a prescribed competence or achievement level in that field may join. Phi Beta Kappa is one such well-known fraternity of this type. These scholastic fraternities are *not* what is being discussed here.

THE TOP TWENTY COLLEGE PRANKS

We could not, in good conscience, write a book on college life without including a list of the top college pranks. For the benefit of both novice and expert jokester alike, we have rated them in the following ways:

Feasibility — This is the difficulty quotient which takes into consideration such things as relative ease of perpetration, the need for exotic materials, time required to execute, number of accomplices, etc.

Risk factor — Since there is an element of risk in all pranks, we have broken this factor down into variables such as likelihood of apprehension, probability of retaliation and the degree of official disapprobation.

Dramatic effect — In many respects the DE is the deciding factor as it alone may determine whether a prank is worth doing. Great dramatic effect may virtually dwarf all other considerations.

All of these variables within the categories are reduced to numerical components and calculated with special formulas to produce a raw score. The scores are plotted on a scale of 1 to 10. For ease of interpretation here is the breakdown:

1-3 = snickers
4-6 = boffo
7-8 = guffaw
9-10 = Le Grande Slam

1. *Old Short Sheets.* Short sheeting goes back to the time of King Tut, but it's still popular, no doubt because it can be used in conjunction with other pranks (slimy biology experiments in the bed, etc.) and easily lends itself to numerous variations. Score: 1

2. *Balloonomania.* Water balloons are perennial favorites. They are cheap, easy to conceal and produce plenty of good-natured fun. One should not underestimate the high degree of dismay a well-aimed water balloon can achieve. Score: 2.5

3. *Novelty Hijinks.* The use of any novelty store paraphernalia as the basis of a prank usually insures success if care is taken to select the right victim. Such props as plastic vomit, whoopie cushions, rubber blood, hot pepper chewing gum, stink bombs, joy buzzers, polyfoam python, squirting boutonniere, etc. are included under this heading. Score: 2.6-3.6

4. *Tub Full of Jello.* This easy-to-perform prank can be a real surprise to the uninitiated, and for that reason it's best practiced on freshmen. Score: 4

5. *High-flying Undies.* Running the victim's underwear up the flagpole is rich in embarrassment potential. Score: 4.2 to 5.2 depending on the relative cleanliness and general condition of the subject's unmentionables.

6. *Bike at Half-mast.* A variation on High-Flying Undies, this one places the victim's transportation up and out of reach. One extra point may be added if the bike is also chained to the flagpole. Score: 4.7

7. *The Kodak Overexposure Exhibition.* Stealing the victim's clothes while she is in the shower is an oldy but a goody. It is easy to perpetrate and takes almost no advance preparation. Add one extra point if the swipe involves more than five victims simultaneously; add two extra points if it is performed in a coed dorm. Base score: 3.8

8. *Time Marches On.* Setting the victim's alarm clock ahead an hour or two brings a bountiful harvest of fun. Best accomplished while the victim sleeps—the night before a test. Make certain to get up with him and go along with it as long as possible—this increases believability. A slightly more complicated variation involves resetting all the clocks in the dorm. Score: 6

9. *When It Rains It Pours.* Unscrewing the lid on the saltshaker is a clever surprise, and fun for the whole table. Overuse, however, seriously limits this prank's appeal, and retaliation is inevitable. Score: 2.9 (Low score typical of food-related shenanigans.)

10. *Kick Me, I'm Yours.* Attaching a ready-made and legible "kick me" sign to the back of the victim can procure hours of delight for a whole campus. The "kiss me" sign variation is also noteworthy. Score: 5

11. *Love Is Deaf.* An intimate phone call to the victim from an anonymous, alluring stranger offers numerous comic possibilities. Add two points if the caller is successful in arranging a date and the victim actually shows up. Score: 5.3-7.3

12. *Mysterious Pizza.* Placing an order for a pizza to be delivered to a nonexistent address is all right, but the effect is considerably heightened when the comestibles are directed to the victim and he is forced to pay for the pizza. Add one extra point for Anchovy Supreme. Score: 5

13. *Vanishing Room.* Boarding up the doorway, plastering and painting it over is a wonderful

prank. Admittedly difficult, it nonetheless produces enormous pleasure whenever it is performed successfully. The cost factor can be considerable, but not out of reach if the whole floor kicks in on it. And if the room is a professor's office—as it was when this prank was successfully performed at Cal Tech in recent years—so much the better. Score: 9

14. *Automotive Magic.* Another Cal Tech favorite, disassembling the victim's car and reassembling it in his room is an all-time winner. Through the years it has taken on slight variations with motorcycles, mopeds and golf carts heisted from security. Great technical skill is required and lots of help, but the payoff is worth it. Score: 8.9

15. *Between a Tree and a Hard Place.* Hoisting the subject's car (VW or other subcompact) and placing it snugly between two trees is close to perfection. The shock of discovery, the amusement of passersby, the victim's futile struggle to free his vehicle all contribute to make this one a doozy. Score: 9

16. *Read All about It.* Stuffing the victim's room full of newspapers floor to ceiling is better than a party. The more people who help, the more fun it is. A dorm classic. Variations include inflating a gigantic weather balloon, or sealing the room with plastic and filling it up with water. With or without the shark, it's priceless. Score: 7.7 and up

17. *Scrambled Cards.* Stealing the code to the card section's display and rewriting your own directions is legendary. This prank takes perfect timing, flawless coordination and inspired brilliance to carry it off, but the results are unparalleled. (A perfect score of 10 if the football game is televised and the card section is viewed over national television.) Score: 9

18. *The Great Stick-Up.* Scotch-taping every single item *on* the victim's desk *to* her desk is great laughs. Imagine her face when she sees that every paperclip, book, pencil, paper, eraser and rubber band has been attached to the desk top—as well as the telephone, typewriter, lamp, dictionary, and notebooks. Score: 6.6

19. *All in a Lather.* An inspired bit of buffoonery, this involves filling a large manila envelope with shaving cream, slipping the open end under the subject's door, and then dropping the largest, heaviest book you can find directly on the bulging envelope. The result is spectacular. A championship prank, at its best when the victim is sitting near the door studying, or talking on the phone. Score: 9.5

20. *The Phantom Student.* A most difficult prank to pull off, but unequaled in effect. It requires the services of a small group of determined hoaxsters who undertake to enroll an imaginary student in a class, take his tests, write his papers, and generally confuse the prof. The ultimate sustained joke. Score: 10

TO TAKE A DRINK

Ah, alcohol. Probably nothing in college is celebrated quite as much as booze in all its various forms. The way some students act you would think they only came to college to get loaded.

All things considered, there is really little good to say about student guzzling—alcoholic beverages don't have much to recommend them. Still, it is for every student to decide personally exactly how to handle the question of drinking. And it's worth spending some time thinking about, because it *is* going to come up; even on campuses where drinking is absolutely prohibited, the opportunity to do so invariably presents itself. Therefore it's best to be prepared.

Here are a few things to consider:

On one hand: Depending on where you go to school, it's almost certain to be illegal for you to drink—for your first couple years, anyway. Drinking under age can get you into a *lot* of trouble, not to mention what will happen if you get caught!

On the second hand: Drinking is highly regulated in most colleges and universities, both off campus and on. There are rules about alcohol which are usually being broken, or at least vastly stretched, by student drinking whenever and wherever it takes place.

On yet another hand: Consumption is usually to excess. Drinking for many students becomes a recreation. To party is to drink. A good time=a good drunk. And since heavy drinking must be done off campus it means driving while intoxicated which is a very good way to get killed or maimed for life.

Many people, Christians most notably, would add a moral contingency to alcohol. Drinking alcoholic beverages is strictly *verboten* for members of many denominations, and outlawed on moral principles on nearly every Christian college campus in the country.

Whether you view a sip of beer as a moral issue or not, you should be aware that there are those around you—from the president of the college on down—who do. It is not your place to claim a special dispensation from school regulations regarding liquor. If it's out for everyone on your campus, it's out for you.

If you are among the many who feel that alcohol is better left in the bottle and that bottle on the shelf, then you really only have one problem: peer pressure. For some inexplicable reason people who are drinking are simply never satisfied unless *everyone* is drinking.

If you should happen to go to a party where everyone is imbibing, you must expect to feel a lot of pressure—and none of it very subtle—to get you loaded. The louder you protest, the more obnoxious the effort to place that glass in your hand.

This type of behavior sometimes comes as a big shock to the uninitiated. Be forewarned. Confronting the lout pushing liquor on you is usually not the answer. Giving in is not the answer either, although an "appearance" of drinking, such as simply holding the same glass all evening, usually is enough to satisfy the most

insistent.

The point is to *know* yourself, to know where you stand on this issue of drinking because it is one place where you are certain to be tested sometime during your years as a student. If you are unsure how you feel you can put off the decision of whether to drink or not until you reach legal age (still twenty-one in some states).

> "Whatsoever weakens your reason, impairs the tenderness of your conscience, obscures your sense of God, or takes off the relish of spiritual things—whatsoever increases the authority of your body over your mind—that thing, to you, is sin."
>
> Susanna Wesley to her son John

If you have foresworn liquor in any form, that's fine. As an underage student you should be applauded. But don't be too critical of your friends who do drink; others may not have your background, maturity or poise. And please don't try to inflict your convictions on anyone else. It never works. You'll be branded as a self-righteous snipe, a goody-twoshoes busybody or a prude. Most likely all three. Just relax and remember that drinking for most students is part of the normal experimentation and curiosity-satisfying process. Your mature example will be enough.

G · R · E · A · T
Dates

You all know about those good cheap dates—movies at the student union, playing video games at the student union, concerts at the student union, having a Coke . . . at the student union.

Needless to say, there are some great dates to be had with a slightly larger monetary investment. Next time you want to do something *really* special, try one of these:

1. ***Dinner for two at the Ritz.*** Pick up your date in a rented limousine (with chauffeur, of course) and enjoy a tantalizing seven-course meal offering the finest in Continental cuisine. Don't forget to make reservations. Price of $350 includes domestic wine (add $70 for French champagne) and the obligatory 15 percent gratuity for the snooty waiter.

2. ***Scalped tickets to the Superbowl.*** $500 includes tickets in the end zone, two pairs of binoculars, hot dogs and soft drinks, a souvenir program and parking fee. Air fare extra.

3. ***A private showing of a movie.*** Depending on what you want, you can lease, for one night's personal use, a print of your favorite film in 16 or 35 mm. Suggestions: *Casablanca, Rocky III, Gone With the Wind, E.T.—the Extra-Terrestrial.* The screen is as big as your wall.

4. ***Hot air balloon ride.*** Bring a picnic lunch and enjoy, enjoy, enjoy while you and your date soar above terra firma in a beautiful balloon. Unless you own your own rig, this will be a chaperoned adventure, but believe me, you won't mind the company. Up, Up, and away!

5. ***Tattoos.*** Plan on a full weekend to complete the process, but you can get nice matching or coordinating tattoos of your choice. Be the envy of your friends and neighbors as you display your dermal artwork. Then head on over to the State Fair; the two of you will have a leg up on the cowboys and cowgirls with their matching Western shirts— kid stuff!

6. ***The ultimate study date.*** Hire Stephen Hawking to tutor you in theoretical physics, John Grisham to help out with your English paper, Pavarotti to give vocal training. How about getting Meryl Streep to help her learn her lines for the one-act on Friday, or having George Gallup come on over and explain random

sampling methods? Don't be afraid to give them a call—these people will do anything for a buck.

7. **_Declare your affection._** A few lovestruck guys have rented billboards and placed their personal message of devotion for the whole world (well, at least everyone who drives down Hollywood Boulevard) to see. But how many do you know who have rented the flashing lights on the Allied Chemical Building in Times Square to pronounce their intent? It won't cost so very much—not more than a few hundred dollars to express your amorous feelings. Of course, you'll have to fly you and your beloved to the Big Apple to view the spectacle. Don't forget to take along a witness or two (with cameras)—they'll never believe you back on campus if you don't. Or consider a full-page, four-color advertisement in _Time_ magazine . . . a spot on television during "Friends" . . . ten 30-second spots on a local radio station.

If you don't have the cash for some of these more exotic dates we will share with you these less expensive outings which we enjoyed.

1. Make dinner for him/her in the dormitory/fraternity house/ sorority house kitchen. Suggested menu: tuna melts, tossed salad with dressing, soft drinks, cookies made from prepared dough.

2. Drive to a nearby small town to go to the show. Try to catch a deliciously bad movie such as _The Legend of Boggy Creek_ or _Wilderness Family._ Bring your own popcorn. Afterward, get a piece of pie at the local drugstore soda fountain; hang out with the locals.

3. Go to one of the special musical programs at a nearby church—the Singing Christmas Tree, or annual _Messiah_ concert, or Sunday School program. Make sure that refreshments are served afterwards!

4. Deliver kiddie valentines to friends on February 14. Visit your favorite profs, friends who live off campus and the dorm mother.

5. After a late night of studying, go out for breakfast at the greasiest highway truck stop you know of. Splurge and get the works—eggs, sausage, hash browns, pancakes on the side and a Coke instead of coffee. Make conversation with the waitress.

6. Oil your chain and plan a long bicycle trip to a nearby beauty spot. Forage for whatever wild foodstuff is available— mushrooms (check with your Botany instructor beforehand), rose hips, wild berries, roots, herbs. Bring back the day's catch and find a way to fix and eat it.

7. Share something you've learned. If you know how to throw a pot, take her to the ceramics lab and let her try it. If you have learned several new European folk dances, show him how they go. Enjoy teaching each other a new skill.

STAYIN' ALIVE: A GUIDE TO CAFETERIA FOOD

Mystery meat: a semi-edible foodstuff that can be prepared and garnished in various ways to create reasonable facsimiles of actual foods. Physical characteristics: flattened, oval shape, approximately 4″ x 5″ x ½″; pressed-wood-type interior covered by sawdust-type exterior; usually fried or steeped in fat; bland, innocuous taste. Possible guises: 1) covered with gravy = "chicken fried steak"; 2) slathered in canned tomato sauce and covered with a cold piece of imitation mozzarella cheese = "veal parmesan"; 3) on a hamburger bun with limp lettuce and tartar sauce = "fish sandwich"; 4) served with creamed, mixed vegetable matter = "Chef's Surprise."

At many schools it is possible to choose from a variety of meal plans. For example, you may want a five-day plan which does not cover weekend meals. Or you can opt for two meals a day (usually lunch and dinner), or get the full twenty meal ticket (very often the food service closes down after the Sunday noon meal). Figure out how many meals you are likely to use, and then get the plan that is most economical for you. You may be able to save money by keeping cereal on hand for light breakfasts in your room, or by fending for yourself on the weekends.

Cafeteria food is notoriously high in starches and fats. There are times when it will seem ages since you've eaten a piece of meat which was not breaded and fried, a vegetable which was not creamed or a dessert which included fresh fruit. Even the milk is most likely whole milk (high in butterfat) and the foods which are presented on an all-you-can-eat basis will be breads, condiments and sweetened fruit drinks. It is not impossible to get a good diet—it's just difficult. Some schools have instituted all-you-can-eat salad bars but even those are populated with potato salad, macaroni salad and thick, fattening dressings.

If you never had to count calories before, you may have to start now. Get a book if you must, but find out the kind of nutrition you are getting (or not getting) in cafeteria foods and their caloric content. Many kids who go away to school just automatically gain ten pounds by Thanksgiving—due, in large part, to the cafeteria offerings.

You can petition the food service to provide more nutritious meals.

A bowl of fresh apples at the end of the serving line is a start; whole wheat bread in addition to white airbread would help; broiled or baked chicken instead of fried chicken provides an alternative for diet-conscious students.

No matter how bad you think the food is, food fights went out

---

25 Least-Liked Foods in the U.S. Armed Forces

1. Buttermilk
2. Skimmed milk
3. Fried parsnips
4. Low-calorie soda
5. Mashed rutabagas
6. French-fried carrots
7. Prune juice
8. Stewed prunes (canned)
9. French-fried cauliflower
10. Creamed onions
11. Kidney bean salad
12. Baked yellow squash
13. Boiled pigs' feet
14. Figs (canned)
15. Carrot, raisin, and celery salad
16. Baked bean sandwich
17. Braised trake*
18. Pickled beet and onion salad
19. Raisin pie
20. Egg drop soup
21. Split pea soup
22. Braised liver with onions
23. Buttered ermal*
24. Chitterlings
25. Sour cream dressing

—From *Chow: A Cook's Tour of Military Food,* by Paul Dickson

*These are nonsense foods listed as a control.

with junior high. Since most of the world is hungry right now, it is inappropriate to waste food by vaulting it across a room full of students.

Cafeteria trays make excellent sleds.

If you need a special diet, you can get food service to provide it. You must contact the food service director prior to the term and let him/her know what your needs are. In most cases they will insist that the great variety (!) they provide as a matter of course should present you with the diet you need, but if you're diabetic or allergic to wheat flour, question that claim vociferously.

The cafeteria will provide a sack lunch when your Art class is having an outing that will run over the lunch hour, or if the Botany class will be out all day gathering specimens. Ask in advance (at least a day or two) what arrangements can be made.

Take a multiple vitamin (and any other supplements you think you need) every day. It will help counteract the unavoidable nutritional deficiencies you will encounter eating cafeteria food.

If you are sick, your roommate can bring you a tray from the cafeteria (if you are certain such an act would not precipitate a worsening of your condition). Call the cafeteria and tell them you're sending her over with your meal ticket and they'll take it from there.

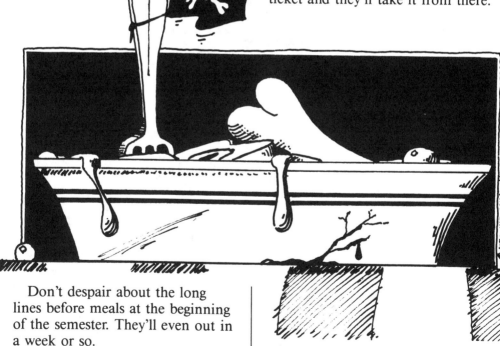

Don't despair about the long lines before meals at the beginning of the semester. They'll even out in a week or so.

In spite of great effort on the part of the administration to facilitate adequate health care, college students almost inevitably suffer from a wide variety of minor illnesses and complaints and a general lack of medical care. Why is this?

Changes

For one thing, you are changing physically. Late adolescence brings about body changes which will make you less susceptible to some diseases and more likely to suffer from others. Depending on your own developmental time clock, your acne may be clearing up or just getting started; you may be over the awkwardness of increased height or just getting there. The sexual changes

YOUR STUDENT

BODY

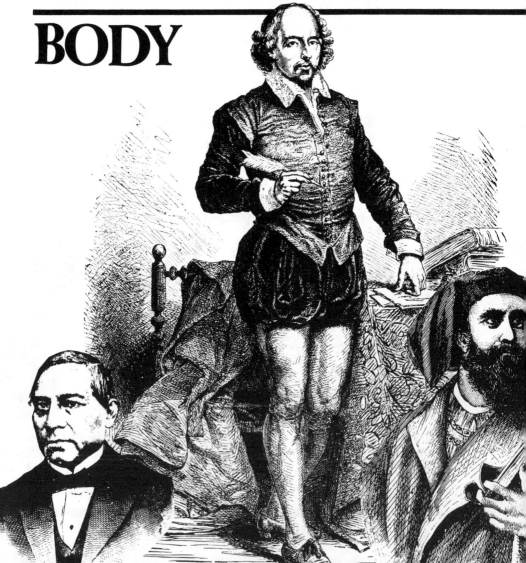

associated with puberty are about over and you find yourself with a body very different than the one you had a few years ago.

Add to all this the simple fact that your life-style has changed. Your previous routine of sleep, eat, work, play—established all through high school and before—is totally recast. Typically, you are getting less sleep, meals and snacks of dubious nutritional content at erratic intervals and more strenuous work and play. Now it's up to you to make sure that you get three good meals a day, that you get to bed at a reasonable hour, even that you brush teeth without being told.

These changes alone can cause problems, and your generally "less healthy" college life-style is a detriment to wellness.

143

The pressures of college life bring about stress, and that can often cause illness too. Students complain about headaches, backaches, exhaustion, lack of energy and depression—most usually related to the increased stress that accompanies difficult studies, pressure for good grades and separation from the support of family and friends. Stress can be a positive, motivating force when it helps you do well in school; it is also a threat to your physical, emotional and psychological well-being.

"I Godda Code Id By Doze"

So you're not feeling well. You have either a general or a specific problem that needs attention. What are you going to do?

Go to the campus health center. This may be a large hospital-like clinic staffed by full-time doctors who provide everything from round-the-clock care for infectious diseases to birth-control information. Or it may be a spare dorm room equipped with first-aid supplies and staffed by the Business Manager's wife (an LPN) who has office hours from 10:00 to 12:00 on Monday, Wednesday, and Thursday. Right away you see that the type of campus health center at your school is going to make a big difference in what kind of problems you take there.

Under certain circumstances you will be very concerned with confidentiality. Even in the large,

very efficient and professional-looking centers your files may be handled by student clerks who have access to their contents. In the small center you can almost count on a personal problem becoming common knowledge. So if you have a condition such as STD or need help with a drug abuse problem, be careful. It's perfectly acceptable to ask, before you go, about the privacy situation.

Larger schools have counseling centers. They are staffed by professional psychologists (who are usually also teachers at the university) equipped to perform a variety of services: vocational, personality, intelligence and psychological testing; psychological counseling; behavior modification classes to quit smoking, eating or develop assertiveness, etc.—to name a few. Even if you believe that your health problem does not directly relate to the services performed by the counseling center, you can get advice about where to go for the help you need.

There are also a number of off-campus resources available to you. Every community has a public health service. Again, the size and competence will vary, but some public health departments have clinics (which are free or low in cost), visiting nurses, drug dispensaries, immunization programs, birth control counseling, detoxification centers and other vital services. You must call them to see what help they offer before you know if that's a viable resource for you.

Local physicians and hospitals may be the best place to go for professional health care. If you have an injury which needs immediate attention, then hightail it over to the hospital emergency room. You will get the immediate care you need and the staff there will make arrangements for necessary follow-up.

Your student health center— large or small—will be able to recommend doctors in various fields whom they have found to be reputable and competent. Or you can call a hospital or the American Medical Association and they will give you a list of licensed practitioners in a given field. Such a referral on their part does not mean that the doctor they refer you to will be sympathetic, inexpensive and look like Trapper John McIntyre. It does mean that he or she is responsible enough to be associated with a local hospital and that the AMA has not kicked him or her out of their fellowship. You can trust a doctor to treat you with complete confidentiality.

Other students can also provide you with leads about good doctors, although you should be careful. A chiropractor who fixed your boyfriend's back and relieved his pain with acupuncture may come highly recommended, but not be the person you need to see for a gynecological problem.

Whether you go to the student health center, counseling center, public health center, hospital or doctor, you will be asked about your symptoms. Be prepared to explain your problem as accurately as you can. If you think it would help, and if you have an opportunity to do so, go to the library and read about your illness a little. Check the *Reader's Guide to Periodical Literature* for magazine articles on various health issues. Or go to the *Journal of the American Medical Association;* keeping a medical dictionary by your side, you will be able to garner more information than you suppose. After a bit of research you will feel more confident when it comes to discussing your condition with a health professional.

Do It!

Getting adequate health care is going to take a great deal of initiative on your part, may cost you money you don't have and could be time-consuming, frustrating and embarrassing. But we can give no better advice than that you should brace yourself to the task and *do it!*

You are the owner of your body and you are responsible for its maintenance and repair. If you have a physical, emotional or psychological problem, get the help you need. Work through your fear and hesitation. If you neglect a problem in its early stages, it could lead to serious consequences. It is never too early or too late to start taking good care of yourself!

Establishing Credit

8

CREDIT
WHERE
CREDIT
IS DUE

There is a secret about getting college credit that colleges don't tell you. We will. It's this: you don't have to go to class to get credit. There *is* another way.

You can, on almost any campus in this country, simply take a test and, providing you pass it, receive credit for the course as if you had sat through a whole term in the classroom. This is called "testing out," and nearly every school has provisions for testing out of certain classes and requirements. In other words, if you can demonstrate ahead of time that you know the material they'll give you the credit for it and you can forget about classes, labs, projects, papers and exams.

Independent organizations offer the tests which can be taken for credit. The best known of these programs is called CLEP, or College-Level Examination Program (brought to you by the SAT and PSAT folks). Another is called PEP—or Proficiency Examination Program.

The use of standardized tests is approved by local colleges and universities who give the actual credit based on their acceptance of your test score.

The benefit? Testing out of a course or two saves you time and money. College is expensive. Why take a class when you already know the subject? Certain lower level college courses duplicate high school subject matter for the benefit of those students who might not have been exposed to it. If you are already a whiz in American History, why take the general survey course? You could test out of it, receive credit, and enter at a higher level. You've saved tuition, a whole term of classes and satisfied the basic degree requirements—you're further ahead from the start.

The testing programs of CLEP and PEP cover general subjects: English, humanities, mathematics, history, social sciences, natural sciences. There are also tests for specific subjects: American Literature, Freshman English, First-year French and German, General Psychology, Algebra, General Biology, Nursing, Criminal Investigation, Trigonometry, Computers and Data Processing, Business Law, Introductory Microeconomics and many more.

CLEP
College Board
P.O. Box 6600
Princeton, NJ 08541

PEP
The American College
Testing Program
Box 168
Iowa City, IA 52243

The tests are not free. The costs vary from less than $100 for entry-level courses, to over $200 for more courses, to as much as $125-$235 for more advanced courses. And tests offered by the school itself are usually based on a percentage of the cost of regular tuition. Any of these is less expensive than actually taking the class in terms of dollars paid; there is the additional saving of shortening your time in college, which means that you are in the work force making money that much sooner.

If you think you might be interested in testing out of a few classes, check with the registrar at your school and find out what tests are offered. For more information about CLEP and PEP write to the addresses in the adjacent box and ask for their program guides.

One final note: check with your school, or with the school you plan to attend *before* taking the exam to make sure they will accept CLEP or PEP test scores for credit. Thousands of schools do, but some do not. The program guides will tell you everything else you need to know.

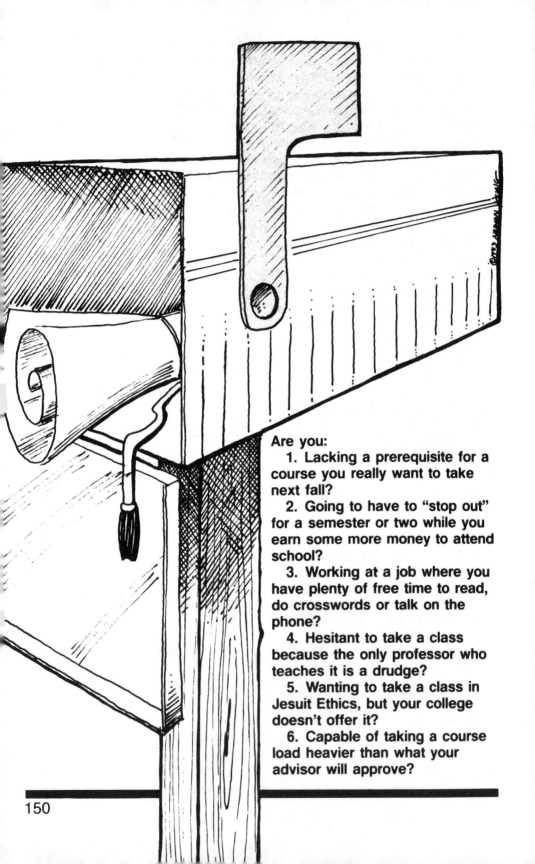

Are you:

1. Lacking a prerequisite for a course you really want to take next fall?

2. Going to have to "stop out" for a semester or two while you earn some more money to attend school?

3. Working at a job where you have plenty of free time to read, do crosswords or talk on the phone?

4. Hesitant to take a class because the only professor who teaches it is a drudge?

5. Wanting to take a class in Jesuit Ethics, but your college doesn't offer it?

6. Capable of taking a course load heavier than what your advisor will approve?

CORRESPONDENCE SCHOOLS

If you answered "yes" to any of these questions, you could be one of many people who could benefit by taking a correspondence course to receive college credit. No, this is not Motel Management by mail. There are dozens of universities across the country offering excellent college training through correspondence school.

These courses are often lower in cost when figured on a credit-by-credit basis. You are given a syllabus, study guide, and assignments to be handed in on a regular basis. You will have a year to complete the course (although you may apply for an extension if you are unable to finish in that time). Your assignments will consist of reading a lesson, studying a text or texts and writing answers to questions that must be submitted and graded by an instructor who will then correspond with you regarding your progress. Some courses may be supplemented by watching programs you see on your local public television station.

It is a fact that most students who begin a correspondence course never finish it. This is probably because of the tremendous discipline it takes to do the work even though no one is taking attendance in class or reducing your grade for every day your assignment is late.

But if you have time you would like to use productively and if you are able to learn well from written material as well as write about what you have learned effectively, it could be just the thing for you.

Want more information? Talk to your advisor or counselor, or check at the bookstore for . . .

Bear's Guide to Earning Non-Traditional College Degrees, by John Bear, Ph.D. Ten Speed Press does it again! This irreverent, exciting guide to degree attainment may change your college plans completely. An excellent source of inspiration, and resource for information.

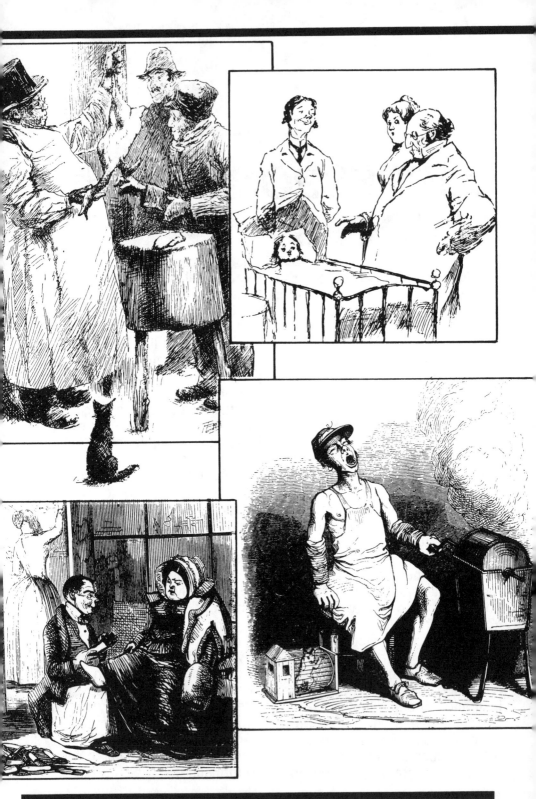

INTERNSHIPS

Internship? You mean like junior M.D.? Dr. Noah Drake? No, like working for little or nothing to get experience in a field you're interested in. Working for a semester or a summer or a whole year on a newspaper staff or for a public-interest lobbying group or at an insurance company. Taking some time off to work at a church to see if you really want to be a youth minister, or sitting in on union negotiations at a large manufacturing plant to observe labor relations from the inside.

Many businesses, branches of local, state and federal government, museums, public service groups and research organizations sponsor internships or fellowships for students who wish to work and learn with them. To get into one of these programs is often one of the best ways to bridge the gap between college and career and to get needed experience before hitting the bricks to find a job.

What It Is

It is on-the-job training. It is sponsored by a group which has work to be done. It is normally unpaid or underpaid. It is sometimes routine, boring clerical work, like filing medical records in a hospital. It is sometimes challenging and eye-opening, like being an assistant to a U.S. Senator, running errands and researching legislative precedents. It

is walking out of the halls of academia, rolling up your sleeves and doing a worthwhile job.

At most colleges it is a way to get credit. It is an opportunity to get education and experience in an area that your school may be weak in. It is a chance to get to know the inner workings of a company with the goal of eventually getting a full-time job with such a company.

How to Find It

The place to go is the library. Look up the *Directory of Internships, Work Experience Programs, and On-the-Job Training Opportunities.* This two-volume manual contains over 600 listings that will help you get started on your search. Listings tell it all—from how much the position pays (if anything) to whether or not it might be an entrée into a full-time job.

But you needn't stop there. Your college placement office is likely to know of local opportunities for internships which might not show up in the directory. These may range from positions with local manufacturing plants to social service agencies in town. Many times you will not need to drop out of school since they are part-time.

If you know of a company you would like to work with, but they do not have an internship program, suggest it yourself. Make an appointment to see the director of personnel or the chief executive officer. Be prepared to tell him or her why you want to work with them, what you have to offer and the terms on which you will work. You may find that your proposal is well received, especially if you are willing to do it for little or no money.

Why should they take you on? Because you will bring fresh ideas and enthusiasm to the job. Because you will work cheap. Because you provide a valuable link between the university and the sponsoring organization. Because you can be on display—with very little risk, the company can look you over with the idea of maybe hiring you in the future. Because hiring you is a community service which will increase their prestige with stockholders, directors and customers.

Many churches and religious organizations will be more than glad to let you work with them even though they have no formal channels for hiring you. Ask your local pastor, or the leader of the Young Life or Campus Life group you attended in high school, or the director of the Greater Metropolitan Fellowship of Churches if they would like to tap your talent. Learn as much about their operation as you can and then come with a plan of duties you might perform. You will receive favored treatment if you come with a willingness to execute a big project they haven't had time to tackle, such as an all-member canvass, a door-to-door survey of church membership in the neighborhood, reorganization of the office record-keeping or establishment of a donor list.

The Christian Colleges & Universities Coalition in Washington, D.C. sponsors the American Studies Program. This semester-long opportunity is open mainly to junior and senior status students who are attending one of the colleges in the Coalition (ask your school administration if that's you). Internships are individually tailored to the student's area of interest and college credit is given by your school for the work you do in Washington. Housing, meals, and supervision are provided. For more information about this program contact the Academic Dean at your college or:

American Studies Program
Christian Colleges & Universities
    Coalition
329 Eighth St. NE
Washington, DC 20002
(202) 546-8713

Getting Credit

Some programs, such as the American Studies Program, provide college credit almost automatically. In other cases you need to take the initiative to get credit. Most sponsoring institutions with established internships will help you get credit by providing an outline of your duties and the time you will spend working that you can pass on to your colleges. Most schools have a method of providing credit for independent study which is done by an upper division student under the supervision of a professor in his major area. Getting credit for your internship comes under this heading. You will probably be required to write a paper concerning your work or present an oral report about your experience.

Check with your advisor, who will give you the necessary guidelines and forms to complete to make your internship show up on your transcript. If you handle it right, you may very well get full semester credit (twelve to eighteen hours) for a semester's work done as an intern. And if you're lucky, they'll pay you a little something to boot! In certain cases you may also apply the financial aid you are getting for your college work to the expenses incurred in the internship. Your advisor can help you figure all this out.

Caveat Emptor

Sounds great, eh? You get off campus for a semester or two, work with the Production Manager of a large public relations firm, dress up for work, are privy to all the big corporate secrets and make a buck on the side.

It's not all roses. You may find yourself in a strange city and very lonely. The small stipend you get may not begin to cover all the extra expenses such as suitable work clothes, food and lodging, transportation and tuition on top of it all. In spite of your careful research into the program, you may find when you get there that you are confined to doing the routine, boring jobs that no one else will touch. Since organizational projects do not necessarily coincide with semester deadlines, you may work for months on a project only to have to go back to school before you see it come to fruition. There may be personality conflicts with the people you work with. There may not be a qualified person to supervise you and show you the ropes.

When you get back to school, you'll feel a little out of it. Perhaps you won't be able to play basketball because you were unable to attend the preseason practices. When you finally get to registration, the classes you need and want are full. Your roommate from last year has a new roomie now, and you're out in the cold. Or you did a lot of growing during your summer in Washington, and your friends don't understand or appreciate that.

You will be less disappointed if you know ahead of time the risks of taking time out to do an internship. But on the whole, even a bad experience will leave you better prepared to bridge that cavernous gap between what you learn in college and what you will be expected to do when you graduate. You'll be way ahead of the game when it comes time to interview with a graduate school or multinational conglomerate if you can point on your resume to your nine months of experience at the Rand Corporation.

So find out what is available, do your research, make your applications and go for it!

Don't Leave home

Without this disaster-thwarting advice

Every year more and more students find the means and desire to flee these native shores and tramp around on foreign soil for a few weeks. Europe, Mexico, South America—no place is safe from the migrating hordes. Most of those trips will end happily ever after. A few will end in disaster.

Everyone encounters little disasters, like missing the last bus to the airport or having six inches of rain on the day reserved for sunbathing on the Riviera. But there are also major disasters lurking which can ruin a whole trip for the unsuspecting globetrotter. Fortunately, most can be prevented if you take a few simple precautions. So, if you plan to travel don't leave until you read this.

Disaster 1: You Lose All Your Money

It's not the worst thing that can happen to you, but it's bad enough. The solution is simple—don't carry money. Instead carry only traveler's checks. If they get lost or stolen they can quickly be replaced (you've heard this before). There are different kinds of traveler's checks, so look around and find out which ones are best for you.

Getting your traveler's checks lost or ripped off is still a hassle you'll want to avoid. Carry them in a safe place—a small pouch around your neck is an excellent idea. Since it is unlikely that you will lose your luggage *and* your money belt *and* your purse *and* your neck pouch, have a few checks stashed in each place to reduce the likelihood of getting completely cleaned out.

You'll need spending money, but be careful not to carry too much. A good idea is to never carry more currency than you can afford to lose. You can exchange your traveler's checks for local currency as you go along; this will help you budget your trip as well, giving you a sort of cash allowance day by day.

An additional tip: exchange your traveler's checks for *small* denominations. You are less likely to be taken advantage of by waiters, taxi drivers and street vendors who make it a practice never to carry change.

If the bottom falls out and you lose all your funds, go to the nearest American embassy or consulate and explain your problem. They know what to do. Another way to get back in the green is to pick up the phone and call home (collect). Ask your friend or relative to go to an American Express or Western Union office and wire you the money. You'll be back in coins in a matter of hours.

Disaster 2: You Lose Your Luggage

The first rule of any traveler is to travel light. Unfortunately, most people take with them about ten times more than they need. Your luggage should include *only* the basic essentials of clothing and personal items. That way, if it's lost or stolen, you aren't ruined and replacing your wardrobe isn't a major undertaking.

The ideal would be to travel with one manageable suitcase and a shoulder bag of some kind. You'll be able to move with freedom (running after trains and buses) and, more importantly, you won't *look like a victim*—a helpless

chicken just waiting to be plucked.

Stick to basic, nondescript luggage, nothing fancy or flashy. Never travel with leather or suede; it doesn't hold up well and it screams MONEY! to any would-be thief. Of course, all your belongings should be tagged with your personal identification and address. You're asking for trouble if it isn't.

The second rule of travel is to lock everything. Lock your suitcase and then lock it in your room. Travel locks that you carry with you provide additional room security for very little cost.

If you exercise the proper precautions and still wind up losing your luggage, tell everyone you can think of. If it was stolen, tell the hotel manager, tell the police (and get the file number of their report), tell your insurance company. If you're traveling with expensive belongings, such as cameras, you should check into some inexpensive traveler's insurance to cover them whether on land, sea or in the air.

Disaster 3: You Get Sick

Travel is tiring and stressful. You're bound to be getting less sleep than normal, eating food your body isn't used to and generally running yourself ragged. Those things alone can cause problems for most people; when you're away from home your troubles are compounded. The word here is: be sensible. Take it easy your first few days abroad and give yourself time to get used to the new routine.

Water is a continual problem for Americans in other parts of the world. Sanitary conditions vary a great deal from country to country, and finding safe, pure water is not always easy. It's not a good idea to go around drinking water—even in a hotel—that you do not know is pure. In some places bottled water may be your only safe bet or ask for cold soft drinks *without ice* (ice doesn't kill bacteria, it merely slows it down). Bring some Tang to make carbonated mineral water more easy to stomach.

Most travelers expect a bout with diarrhea and pack something to either prevent Montezuma's Revenge or stop it if it does catch up to them. Any qualified pharmacist will be able to recommend a suitably potent brand.

Your doctor should be notified of your travel plans. Tell him where you are going; he'll know whether you need shots or not. He'll also be able to recommend some useful medicines you can take with you "just in case." Of course, if you have any particular allergies or hay fever, take along your cure. Medicines are different in other countries and likely to be more expensive than here. Anyway, you won't want to waste any time running around to foreign drugstores when you could be sightseeing. Do bring your prescription, though, just in case you run out of essential medications.

Disaster 4: You Get Put in Jail

Getting into serious trouble is the last thing on your mind, but sadly enough, it happens. Especially now, when most of the world is concerned about drug traffic and smuggling, teenagers and young people can be picked on for little or no reason. You should know that the rest of the world's drug laws— even regarding marijuana—are more strict than our own.

Stories circulate about students who have unknowingly smuggled drugs merely by accepting a ride across a border, and have wound up in jail for twenty years. It happens. Therefore, be on your best conduct and behavior at all times. And stay far away from *any* questionable activities or shady situations.

Americans are not immune to the laws of a foreign country. When these come into play, you're on your own. *Do* contact the U.S. Ambassador or American Consul if you are arrested. He can't get you off the hook merely by waving the American flag, but he'll protect whatever legal rights you possess. There are also international student organizations for each place you'll be visiting.

When disaster strikes don't panic. Remember who your friends are and swallow your pride and ask for help. There are many sources of aid close to the traveler in trouble, whatever it may be. Send out your S.O.S. and most likely you'll be sailing smooth again in no time.

Reprinted with permission. © 1978 by CAMPUS LIFE Magazine, Youth for Christ.

HOW TO READ
STUDY-ABROAD
LITERATURE

By Lily von Klemperer*

*Reprinted with the permission of the Council on International Educational Exchange, Institute of International Education, and the National Association for Foreign Student Affairs. Reprinted from NAFSA Newsletter, December 1976.

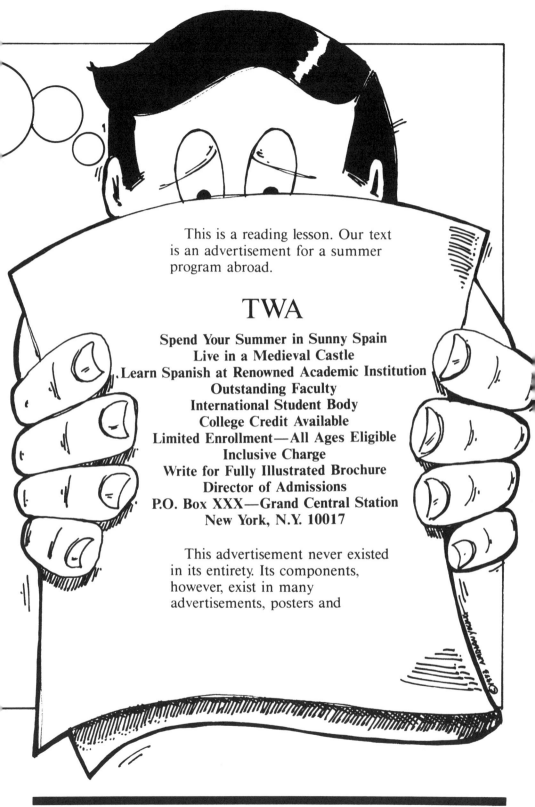

This is a reading lesson. Our text is an advertisement for a summer program abroad.

TWA

Spend Your Summer in Sunny Spain
Live in a Medieval Castle
Learn Spanish at Renowned Academic Institution
Outstanding Faculty
International Student Body
College Credit Available
Limited Enrollment—All Ages Eligible
Inclusive Charge
Write for Fully Illustrated Brochure
Director of Admissions
P.O. Box XXX—Grand Central Station
New York, N.Y. 10017

This advertisement never existed in its entirety. Its components, however, exist in many advertisements, posters and brochures. Advertisements and posters may have to be somewhat flashy and overstated to catch the eye. Brochures, on the other hand, have to be factual, realistic—and totally honest. Let us analyze the components of the sample ad. This will remind us how to read and interpret descriptive literature on study programs abroad, and what questions to ask ourselves and others.

1. Is there a name of a responsible person or just a title— or not even that? A covering letter ending "Yours truly, Director of Studies" (no signature) makes you wonder. If you then search the "fully illustrated brochure" and find no board of advisors, no trustees listed—no names whatsoever— what conclusions would you reach?

2. Is there an address or just a P.O. box number? How can one get hold of them in an emergency? Wouldn't parents expect to see an address? (And a P.O. box number in Ann Arbor does not necessarily imply University of Michigan sponsorship.)

3. Is the institution abroad identified or is it referred to as "famous university," "recognized academic institution," or "accredited university"? Why don't they give the name of the institution? Foreign universities, suspend their regular operation during the summer months. Do they possibly refer to a special course for foreigners *at* one of the universities? Might the "famous university" be Oxford in summertime, when its colleges are available to anyone willing to pay

the rent? If they use the terms "accredited" and "recognized"— accredited or recognized by whom?

4. If they say "earn X semester hours credit" or "credit available," who makes it available? Have you looked to see whether your institution is listed among "the following institutions have in the past given credit to students who have attended our program"? Does anybody recall the circumstances under which a student at some time or other may or may not have been given credit?

"Cauliflower is nothing but cabbage with a college education."

Mark Twain
Pudd'nhead Wilson's Calendar

---

5. If we read "outstanding faculty" or "famous professors," why are we not given their names, rank and affiliation? Who are they? Where did they get their degrees? Where do they teach? What do they teach?

6. If you see the professor's name in large print and that of the U.S. university in small print, and if the advertisement of the brochure is "crowned" by TWA or a similar commercial identification, whose program is it? Does PAN AM give the credit? Is anyone getting a free trip?

7. If they say "all ages eligible" or "congenial student body," how

homegeneous is a program "open to college students, high-school students, teachers, professors and professionals"? Does "credit optional" make for a cohesive group? Some work for credit and many don't?

8. If they indicate "limited enrollment" why is there continuous publicity and the suggestion to "call collect"? Why do they send a form letter in March saying that the May deadline has been extended to June? Doesn't limited enrollment presuppose selectivity? Does "your application will be reviewed as soon as it is complete, and you will be promptly notified of your acceptance or rejection" bespeak selectivity?

9. If an "international student body" is advertised, let us look a bit more closely at the roster of students in the back of the brochure. Is Joe Doe from Brussels a Belgian? Is Mary Smith from Ankara a Turk? Are they swelling the ranks of "international students" by listing—you guessed it—the children of U.S. parents who are serving abroad?

10. "Spend your summer in sunny Spain." "Learn Spanish." Sun and fun? Learn while you sun? Have fun while you learn? Learn what? You certainly have to look very carefully at the balance there. How prominent is the learning part, how convincing is the curriculum? How many hours of what? Who teaches what, where, and when?

11. How romantic!—"a medieval castle"! But is it near that "famous university"? Is it near inexpensive eating places? Are there adequate rooms or six people to a room in the former servants' quarters? If family living is suggested, is it a family that likes to have foreign students stay with them or is it a crotchety old lady who likes their dollars? Is whatever housing offered close to the center of town and cultural events? Is there transportation after 6 P.M. or do students have to rely on expensive taxis?

12. A crucial question is: What is meant by "inclusive charge"? There are almost as many variations as there are programs. The most important thing for you is to find out what is not covered. Read the small print. How big is the nonrefundable application fee? Do you pay for a three-week program including the first and last weekend? What happens during vacation time? Is there an estimate of total expenses?

13. This gets us to the last item, the "fully illustrated brochure." Organizers of high-quality programs do not normally publicize them with snow-topped mountains, bathing beauties, flamenco dancers, the spires of Oxford plus a breezy travel folder text.

Descriptive literature on foreign study should reflect the serious intent of the organizers. It should reflect quality, selectivity and effective academic control. A meaningful and solid program cannot accommodate all tastes, all needs, all levels of social maturity. But whatever it is meant to represent should be stated with honesty.

OVER THERE:

There are limitless sources of information for the student who wishes to travel abroad. Whether you intend to get college credit for your sojourn, or simply wish to eat sauerbraten or drive on the left-hand side of the road, you'll benefit from gathering as much information as you can before you leave. After all, traveling is exciting enough without getting stopped at the Turkish border because your visa isn't in order.

The following resources might be helpful:

1. *Your friendly neighborhood travel agent.* You don't have to be booking a seat on the Concorde to get their help. And it doesn't cost you a penny more to book with a travel agent—it's the airlines, hotels, and railways who pick up the tab. Make the travel agent your first stop when planning any overseas trip; they are privvy to the latest and best information on fares, travel documents, exchange rates, emergency services, and available accomodations.

2. *The Council on International Education.* This non-profit agency is the largest U.S. higher educational exchange agency—and an excellent source of information if you plan to study abroad. If you write to them, they will send you a brochure of their publications: everything from how to tour South Africa if you're a performing artist, to applying for a Fulbright Scholarship.

ACCESS TO INFORMATION

Write to:

Council on International Education Exchange
205 E. 42nd Street
New York, NY 10017-5706

Ask for their most current publications listing or contact their website at http://www.ciee.org/.

3. *The U.S. State Department.* Uncle Sam has a hot line which issues up-to-date advisories for travelers abroad. You'll get information on civil strife, epidemics, medical conditions, and political situations for many countries and areas. The advisories are kept up-to-date, so you'll always get the latest scoop. If you're planning to travel in or even near a known trouble-spot, spend a dime and make the call. The hot line is open from 8:15 a.m. to 5:00 p.m. (EST) on weekdays. If you have a touchtone phone, call the number twenty-four hours a day for a recorded advisory. And the number to call is . . .

(202) 647-5225

Also available from the State Department's Bureau of Consular Affairs are many publications, including a series of booklets, "Tips for Travelers." Titles and featured countries vary from time to time. There is a

"We need to liberalize vocational education— and vocation-alize liberal education."

Terrene H. Bell

165

small charge for each booklet, and you can request them from . . .

Superintendent of Documents
U.S. Government Printing Office
Washington, DC 20402

or contact their website at http://travel.state.gov/.

4. *U.S. Customs Service.* Their little pamphlet "Know Before You Go" will guide you through the customs process. And you should, indeed, know before you go all about import restrictions, duty free regulations, exemptions, declarations and possible tax liabilities. This pamphlet is widely available from travel agents, or can be obtained from . . .

U.S. Customs
P.O. Box 7407
Washington, DC 20044

Ask for Publication No. 512.

5. *Libraries and the Internet.* Your school or public library and the Internet are also good sources of information about overseas travel and study. The important thing is this: get the most information you can, and make sure it's current.

Special Relations

You're married? Going to get married? Still in school? Well, there's . . .

GOOD NEWS AND BAD NEWS

The good news is that you're lucky to have found your life's companion: the perfect person to support and encourage you during your studies.

The bad news is that she is going to take up a lot of your time, if you want this marriage to be successful.

The good news is that there are a lot of things you can do together to help each other. You can study together (when both of you are students), quiz each other, cheer each other on. You're not alone!

The bad news is that you're not *ever* alone. Those 3 A.M. cram sessions aren't going to go over real big when he's counting on you to drive him to work at 6:45 the next morning. And you have responsibilities around the house, too. There's trash to take out, and dishes to wash and supper to get ready.

The good news is that supper is under your control now. No more "Chef's Special" at the cafeteria. If you want to have breakfast at 10:15 when food service is closed then you can jolly well have it. And you're convinced that it will be cheaper to do all your own cooking.

The bad news is that even if you can eat for less, this marriage will generate its own expenses. There's life insurance and health insurance and the deposit on the apartment and furniture and commuting expense, not to mention the regular student-type expenses of books and tuition and fees.

The good news is that if one of you is working to put the other one through, you may find yourself in a better financial situation than you were when you were single. On the other hand, if you are really needy (especially if you're both in school) you might qualify for all kinds of assistance that you didn't before, like grants, loans, good on-campus jobs—and your parents might be willing to continue to contribute something toward your school expenses even though you've left the nest.

The bad news is that, having left the nest, you are faced with new responsibilities. You must manage the money, keep your grades up and still find time to spend with each other, because that's why you got married in the first place.

The good news is that you *have* time together. Since you're eating and sleeping and generally living together you don't have to steal odd moments the way you did when you were dating—like skipping class to have a talk or staying up until 4:00 A.M. the night before the Econ mid-term discussing wedding plans!

The bad news is that your worlds may be very different now. She's working as a credit supervisor at the bank, wearing nice suits to work and having lunch with the management team. You're wearing Levi's and your Air Force parka while you pedal your ten-speed to class, and you're taking courses like Physical Geography, Human Ecology and a seminar in Political Problems. So what do you have in common?

The good news is that you can bring something exciting and new home to each other at the end of the day. He may get bored balancing books all day, and you're not exactly living in the real world with your three P.E. classes, one Art lab and an English course to occupy your time. You have the opportunity to share what you've learned and experienced each day, adding spice to the relationship.

The bad news is that your involvement in the other's activities is almost certain to keep you from participating in a lot that the school has to offer. It's going to be harder to get to the student recitals, afternoon track meets, lectures by special speakers—not to mention the library, biology lab and chapel—when it means driving or riding your bike a mile or so instead of walking from the dorm.

The good news is that you don't live in the dorm anymore. No crummy roommate stealing your pens, no stereos turned up to "9" playing Conway Twitty, no hours, no walking to the end of the hall just to brush your teeth.

The bad news is—no fun! No college fun. You're really still just a kid and you've made this big decision and for better or worse that's the way it is. Life is more serious now. There are responsibilities. There are commitments. There are sacrifices.

The good news is that if you are married, and you are still in school, there are many things that you can do to create a good marriage and make your college experience rewarding. While many "authorities" caution against getting your Mrs. degree before your B.A. degree (mostly because that means an early marriage which has a higher mortality rate than a later marriage), you may find that it's the best decision you ever made. Here are some suggestions for keeping it all together:

1. If possible, schedule your classes and do your studying while your spouse is at work. If you apply yourself, and approach college like a 9-5 job, you can pretty much get your work done while your husband or wife is doing his/hers. This way you will have more time together to pursue mutual interests.

2. Have a party. Invite her friends from work and yours from school. Keep in mind that these people may not have much in common to begin with, but everyone likes a party; in addition to having a good time, you'll get a glimpse of the other's world.

3. Go to his office Christmas party and bring him to your school homecoming. Play on the factory's softball league with him but swim at the college pool. The idea is for the student spouse to get *off* campus and for the working spouse to get *on* campus.

4. Develop common interests together that are not especially work or school related. Attend church together, work for a local political candidate, make a piece of furniture, jog or exercise together. For a while put aside your different "occupations" and concentrate on your mutual goal.

5. Talk, talk, talk. If you're feeling angry because you worked hard all day while he spent three hours with his professor discussing Barth and Sartre, and now supper isn't ready (he knew you were working late and needed his help!), say so. Don't stew about it. And if you must study tonight, and were counting on her to help quiz you on those chemistry formulas, but she's going to a home decorating party that one of the other nurses is having (there's no money to buy any of that junk!), it's best to get it out in the open and discuss it.

Throughout your married life you will have many roles, and they will change. Right now you are a student and he is a surveyor. Later you may be working while he goes to graduate school. When and if you have children, one of you may decide to stay home and take care of them while the other works. After they're grown your roles will change again. It's really not so unusual or such a hardship to be married while in school. You must develop communication skills now which will be used constantly in the years ahead; you must develop maturity to deal with some difficult situations. But you will be rewarded with the special intimacy which comes only by sharing your life with another person you love.

PARENTS

Going Home For Vacation

When I was ten, my oldest brother went away to a small Christian school in the Midwest to begin his college education. The entire family was proud of him. He was the oldest, the smartest, the most motivated of all the children, and we looked up to him.

He came home for the first time at Thanksgiving, and presto chango!—our favorite sibling had turned into an intolerable bore. Part of this was attributable to a freshman psychology course he had been taking. If one were to ask him, for example, how he felt about the NFL Superbowl race this year, he would reply, "Well, how do *you* feel?" And if, as a fifth grader, I innocently remarked that all teachers were creeps, he would retort, "That's a rash generalization and a dogmatic statement. You have no possible way of knowing if all teachers past and present, all over the world, are creeps. Define creep, if you will."

In spite of this puzzling behavior, we did want to spend some time with him. But he was no sooner home than he was gone again. Being with the family was not as important to him as seeing his girlfriend and playing basketball with high school buddies he hadn't seen since summer.

Even at the tender age of ten I knew this wasn't right. So I asked him to go on a walk with me, and he obliged. He now recalls that I worked him over pretty good, explaining that his freshman psychology wasn't very popular with the old folks at home, and that if he wanted to stay in the warm bosom of his family, he'd better rethink how he was treating us and remember that we knew him *when;* that his college airs didn't deceive or impress us one bit.

Believe it or not, almost twenty years later, he still remembers he was grateful.

But *you* don't want to have to hear it from your little sister. That's the painful way; so here is some advice to help you through those visits home:

1. Your parents are spending thousands of dollars on your education. You are their child. They'd like to know how it's going. At the very least you owe them a nice long sit-down visit about your classes, your professors, the activities you are involved in and an indication of what you are learning. If you are having some problems, this is a good time to let them know. If you need more money or you can't stand living in the dorm another minute or if you think you'll need to take a lighter course load next semester or if you're really homesick and thinking about transferring to Hometown Junior College, talk about it. Let them know you still value their opinion and appreciate their support.

2. If things seem different when you go home for the first time, it is most likely you who has changed. Your parents and family want you to change and grow, but may be dismayed at what they actually see. If Mom and Dad are long-time Democrats and you come back as president of Young Republicans, that situation will need to be handled with tact. You are entitled to your own life but remember that they expect you, in general, to emulate their values. Don't rub their noses in your fancy new ways.

3. They want you around them during your vacation but you want to be with your friends. A good solution is to ask your folks if you can have some of your pals over one evening. From a practical point of view, having the gang at your place is a more efficient way of getting to see everyone and your family will appreciate it. At any

rate, talk to your parents and let them know that it's important to you to see your friends, and then work something out that is agreeable to all of you.

4. While you've been at school you've had no set hours, complete freedom to do whatever you wanted and no one looking over your shoulder. It doesn't take long to get used to this and cherish it. But you're at home now, on your parents' turf. Respect the fact that they'll probably still wait up for you and will want to know where you are. It won't kill you to play the game again for a few days.

Living at Home

You are going to school in your home town. If it is a junior college, there may be no on-campus housing, and even if the school does have dorms, you find the cost prohibitive. And what's the point of living in a cramped little room and eating rotten food when there's plenty of space for you at home (so argues Mom)?

If you are living at home, your parents are likely to view your college years as a continuation of your high school days. Nothing much has changed as far as they are concerned.

But things have changed for you; you need more freedom, you need to expand, you need to grow. You are preparing for life on your own.

So take your parents out for dinner or a Coke or whatever and explain this to them. Explain that there will be adjustments to make

in the way you relate to each other. Explain that you do need their financial support, you do need to live in their home, but you also need greater freedom. Iron out any difficulties that you can foresee before they become big issues: "If you think you're so smart, Mr. College Student, then you can just pay your own tuition! And you can pay rent here, too. I don't make hot meals every night to have you come waltzing in unannounced at 9:30 wanting something to eat. You can eat with the rest of the family or go without!"

Don't let this happen to you.

The Visiting Dignitaries

Your family is from Montpelier, Vermont and you're going to school at the University of Hawaii; some day (under the circumstances, probably in February) your folks are going to call or you're going to get a letter saying that they're coming for a visit. You get a pain in your chest. There's a beer can collection growing on your window sill. When they find out what a radical Professor Jensen is, they'll pull you out of school for sure. What if they want to visit the frat house? What if they bring Janie? All the guys will think your little sister is a nerd, because she is. Where are they going to stay? They can't stay in the dorm! When will they leave? Why are they coming here in the first place? Don't they trust you?

Calm down. Here's what to do:

1. Prepare for their visit the day you leave home. Your parents are going to want to see what things are like for you at school. They aren't prying, they aren't stepping out of bounds. They are merely curious, and they have a right to be. You're still their little girl. If you have made some life-style changes that they won't approve of, you should be breaking it to them gently all along.

2. Once you get the news, call them back or write and ask for any details that they may not have given you yet. You need to know when they are arriving and when they plan to leave. Sleeping arrangements must be made. Your dorm or frat house or apartment may have room for them, but it would probably be better to have them stay at a nearby motel. Most student living quarters are barely adequate for the student, much less additional family members. *You* are the host; *you* decide where they will stay.

3. Look at your schedule and budget your time. Let them know, before they come, what hours you must be in class, at work and studying. They should not come with the mistaken notion that you will be their full-time "cruise director." You are a student first and tour guide second. In the main, they will be glad to see you so diligent about your academic obligations.

4. Plan activities to occupy their time while you are busy with school. Get pamphlets from the local Chamber of Commerce, ask your friends, check the newspaper for coming events. If your mother is a school librarian, go to the college library and ask if they would give her a tour while she's there. If your dad is an orthodontist, he might want to sit in on some lectures at the College of Dentistry. Most faculty and staff, if notified in advance, will be happy to help out.

5. Arrange for your parents to meet your friends. They want to know who you're hanging around with. If your roommates play golf and your dad is a devotee, arrange an outing. Find some common ground between them. If nothing else, everyone would probably enjoy going out for a pizza or ice cream sundaes some evening. No fooling, they will enjoy meeting each other.

You may be worried that your friends will think your parents are dumb. Maybe so; they also think their own parents are dumb. You're all in the same boat. Chances are that your folks are pretty much like everyone else's; so try not to worry about it.

6. Your mom and dad would like to attend a class with you. If you're a little shy about this, pick a large class where there is a certain anonymity. Or a small one where you'll feel comfortable amongst a lesser number of people. Choose a class that they will be interested in (stay away from your ultra-technical upper-division classes in virology, for example). Introduce them to your instructor either before or after class. This will go over big with your teacher and your folks.

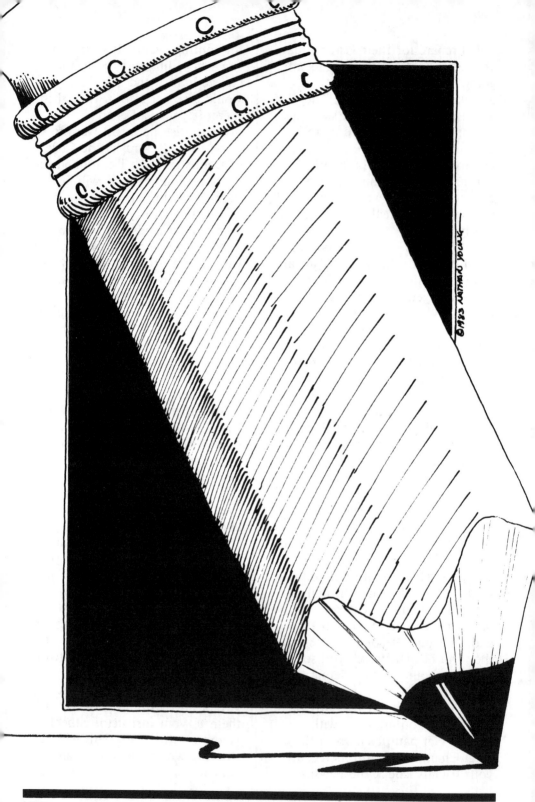

CREATIVE PENMANSHIP: THE LOST ART OF LETTER WRITING

Sure, it's easy to write home when all you have to say is that you made the Dean's List or that you've tested out of your sophomore year. But some news isn't so easy to break.

Dear Mom and Dad:

I'm $orry that it'$ taken $o long for me to write to you. I had every intention of doing $o earlier, but there have been a lot of thing$ to do and I gue$$ I ju$t got bu$y.

Ye$terday I wa$ at the book$tore trying to de¢ide whether or not I $hould get the E¢onomi¢$ textbook or put ga$ in my ¢ar $o that I ¢an get to ¢la$$. That wa$ a tough de¢i$ion to make. In the end I de¢ided to put the money on a¢¢ount with the Bur$ar, who ha$ been writing me a lot of threatening letter$ about what I owe the $¢hool for fee$ that I wa$n't able to pay.

Well, that'$ about all for now. I $ure do like to hear from you. Mom, we all liked the ¢ookie$ you $ent; maybe next time you ¢ould put a few ¢an$ of $pam in the mail. That would be great.

Love, Jerry.

Dear Daddy and Mother:

Hey, I'm really excited! You know that I have been looking for a part-time job to help pay for some of the things I think I need but that you think I could do without since it's costing so much already to go to this school. Well, I think our problem is solved!

Yesterday I saw an ad in the paper for a hostess at a cozy little place close to campus, so I went over and the man, Mr. Vito, was real nice. He said that I would be just perfect. He asked if I liked to dance, and I said sure, and he wanted to know if I liked people, and I said gee, I *love people,* so he hired me! It's a great job—I don't have to be at work until 10 at night, and I can quit around 4:00 A.M. I can study after that, eat breakfast, and make it to my 7:30 classes. Neat, huh?

All the girls—there are about a dozen in all—wear these cute little kitty cat outfits. Real spiffy!

Anyway, all I have to do is just slink around and mingle with the customers, dance with them if they want to dance, and generally make them feel welcome at the club. It's incredible how friendly the customers are!

Gotta go now. There's a guy at the door with a package. Maybe it's my outfit! No—I don't think so . . . the box looks way too small.

Well, don't worry about me. As you can see, I've got my money problems licked. Isn't that super? Now you won't have to send me the money I asked for in my last letter.

Ciao!

Love, Cindy

P.S. You wouldn't believe what a girl can make in tips!

Dear Dad:

How are you? I'm fine.

I've got some great news: I'll be home a little ahead of schedule this spring. It looks like I'll be able to finish before the term is up. I talked to the Dean of Students yesterday, and he didn't see any reason why I shouldn't just go ahead and leave for home even though there are another couple of months left in the semester. Basically, I think it has something to do with some fraternity functions I've been involved in that made him think that I might just want to wrap things up here at college in a day or two.

I'm really glad that now I'll have a chance to get a head start on the summer job situation.

I know you weren't expecting me until the end of May, but it's not like you've rented out my room or anything, right? (ha, ha) No need to meet me at the bus next Saturday . . . I'll just thumb a ride to the house. Love to Mom.

Kirk

Dear Mummy:

Mummy darling, you're going to get a simply *awful* notice from State in a few days, and I want you to just *ignore* what you get because it's really *nothing* to get alarmed about.

It seems that the registrar (she's just a dear, but *really*, Mummy, she's so old and confused that I don't know *why* they keep her on!) has misrecorded *everything* that the professors sent her, and she has *mistakenly* gotten it into her head that I'm not doing very well here, and she's going to send you some little pink slips that say all sorts of *horrible* lies about my grades.

> ## "It is not uncommon to hear sophomores and juniors in college reassuring the freshmen that parents are not really so bad as they seem, and in fact may become rather interesting people."
>
> Frederick W. Coons

Have you ever *heard* such a silly thing? So, don't pay a *bit* of attention to what you get by post, Mummy. I'll get it *all* cleared up and set the records straight.

Remember now, Mummy, you just *ignore* it—don't even *open* the envelope. It doesn't mean a thing, and even if I *could* be doing a little better, by the time *final* grades are out, the whole thing will be *straightened out,* I promise.

Love and smooches!
Muffy

Dear Mom and Dad:

I got your letter saying that you were going to come and visit me here at school. Gee, that's nice.

I'm trying real hard to find a decent place for you to stay. You wouldn't want to stay here in the dorm, because they said that they're going to be spraying for roaches and rats the whole month of May. That might be kind of hard on Mom's allergies.

The nearest motel isn't a great place, but I suppose it'll do. The only problem is that they charge by the hour, usually, but I'm going to call the No-Tell Motel and see if we can't get some kind of day rate for you guys.

I hope that we'll have some time to do something when you're here. Since I'm studying about fifty hours a week on the average, plus my part-time job and classes, it'll be kinda hard to get together. Maybe we can have breakfast together some morning?

I really am looking forward to seeing you, even though I am coming home at the end of May and we'll have the whole summer to talk, so I really can't understand why you're choosing now to come. Anyway, I'm sure that your trip will be a lot of fun. I'll do everything I can to make your accommodations as good as they can be for you.

Love, Jim
P.S. Is Cathie coming, too? Do you think that's wise? I mean, doesn't she have to study or something? When I was her age you couldn't get out of school for your own funeral!

Keeping Faith

10

RELIGIOUS ORGANIZATION

If you are attending a church-related or Christian school you will be presented with ample opportunity to meet with other students who are interested in sharing and developing their faith. If you are at a state university, however, it may be more difficult to find others of like faith and spirit. This inability to make contact can make you lonely and confused. As a Christian, you need the day-to-day support of other students and faculty who are Christians and want to integrate their faith with learning.

Do not fail to fill out the religious preference card which is enclosed in your registration materials. Most universities cooperate with campus organizations in the use of these cards, which indicate your religious background. The cards are collated and passed on to the appropriate group and that group—depending upon its degree of fervor—will contact you during the first part of the semester. Don't be afraid to talk

to them; they aren't going to pressure you into something you aren't interested in. For the most part they just want to let you know that they are around and that you are invited to join them.

Below are listed the organizations that are most likely to be on state university campuses (many of them are present on Christian campuses, too). If a group that you are interested in is not visible on your campus, you can write to their national office and ask them to put you in touch with a nearby group or help you form a new one. The national organization of your home church's denomination can help, too. Ask your pastor.

Southern Baptist: The Baptist Student Union is present on almost every university campus south of the Mason-Dixon and on most that are north, too. This well-organized, aggressive denomination will probably contact you one way or another and invite you to be a part of their group,

S

which stresses participation in a local church and membership in on-campus BSU groups that provide Bible study, service projects and a variety of other opportunities. National Office:

National Student Ministries
127 Ninth Avenue North
Nashville, TN 37234

Protestant and Catholic Ministries: On many colleges and university campuses you'll find separate denominational ministries, or a cooperative organization that represents several mainline Protestant denominations (United Methodist, Christian Church/Disciples of Christ, United Presbyterian, etc.). It will have a name such as *United Campus Ministries*. The Newman Centers and Aquinas Centers offer programs for Catholic students.

Many centers offer Sunday worship services, support and Bible study groups, and social outings. They are often very involved in social action and political causes. Since groups vary so much from campus to campus, check out the local scene for yourself.

InterVarsity Christian Fellowship: This nondenominational organization has made a commitment to evangelism on college campuses. It emphasizes Bible study and fellowship among Christian students and has programs which encourage students to consider a broad view of what they might do after graduation—the Urbana conferences, for example, which stresses opportunities in missions. They are one of the largest

para-church organizations on college campuses.

Do investigate InterVarsity. In doing so you'll plug into a nationwide—an *international*—network of Christian students who are taking seriously the challenge to be operative in the real world.

If you are unable to make contact with IVCF on your campus, write for information:

InterVarsity Christian Fellowship
6400 Shroeder Road
Box 7895
Madison, WI 53707-7895

or, in Canada . . .

InterVarsity Christian Fellowship
40 Vogell Road
Unit 17
Richmond Hill, Ontario L4B 3N6

Campus Crusade for Christ: You may know CCC because of their popular *Four Spiritual Laws* and the large-scale evangelistic campaigns. They have an outreach emphasis to their work on college campuses. In addition, they sponsor seminars, Bible studies and special retreats and conferences. Their aim is to encourage students to be totally committed to leaving the mark of Christ on their school and the world. If you share this vision, you may wish to join them. Write:

Campus Crusade for Christ
  International
100 Sunport Lane
Orlando, FL 32809

The Navigators: Another organization which is committed to

converting students and involving them in Bible study and fellowship with other Christians. Their publishing arm, NavPress, has put out some excellent books. They also offer training seminars at their headquarters in Colorado Springs. If you are unable to find the Navigators on your campus (highly unlikely, if they are there) write:

Navigators
Box 6000
Colorado Springs, CO 80934

The YMCA and YWCA:

The Young Men's Christian Fellowship, in most instances, has lost its religious emphasis over the years and is now known mostly for recreational programs. There may be an active YMCA or YWCA near your college. Even though the organization no longer stresses Christianity per se, this is still a good place to make contact with other people who are interested in spiritual issues.

Local Churches:

Don't overlook the local churches in town. Most of these will bend over backward to make it easy for you to attend services. They can arrange for someone to pick you up for church and many plan special activities for college students. Some have programs where a family in the church will "adopt" a student. Jump at the chance, if you get it. It means good Sunday dinners and the warmth of people who care about you.

If you went to your parents' church all your life, you may be unsure about how to get involved in a new church where you are unknown. Start out by attending Sunday school and church one morning (one *Sunday* morning). Attending both shows that you are serious about finding a church home. If you think it's a place you might like, register your attendance on a pew card. Then, take a deep breath and talk to the person next to you after the service. Believe me, when you let them know that you are a college student who is looking for a church to attend, they will be absolutely delighted and fall all over themselves to welcome you. Some churches have what they call "watchcare membership" for students and temporary residents who want to retain their home church membership but would also like to be a part of the church in their away-from-home community.

CULT WATCH

Not all religious organizations on campus will be helpful to you; not all will even be legitimate. Virtually every college campus is a prime recruiting ground for many of the cults which are trying to snag college-age young people into their "fellowship."

You may argue that it is not fair to label religious groups with the now-derogatory term "cult" simply because they do not conform to the ideals of mainstream Christianity, and that is true. A group should not be condemned simply because it is newly formed or a little offbeat in its practices. But before you get involved in any religious group, examine the following:*

Techniques of conversion: Does the group bring about conversion and compliance through emotional and/or physical manipulation? Do new members get enough sleep, enough food, adequate privacy?

Leadership: Does the leader of the group claim to be the Messiah? Does the leader claim to be the *only one* who can correctly interpret Scripture and religious writings? Is the leader wealthy in excess?

Authority: Are members required to obey orders blindly? May they question directives from the leader?

Legal posture: Does the group claim to be immune from the proscriptions of the laws of society? Does it carry on activities in the name of God which are counter to the letter and spirit of civil law?

Finances: Again, is the leader wealthy? Are members required to give all their personal possessions to the group? If a member leaves the group, will she get her investment back? Are members required to spend an inordinate amount of time doing solicitation and fund-raising? Is such fund-raising done in an ethical and legal way?

Sociology: Are members required to sever their ties with parents, friends, siblings, spouses? Are dating and marriage restricted or forbidden? Are women exploited?

Politics: Is the group politically motivated? Is world domination or world change a goal of the group?

Exclusive thought systems: Are members of the group allowed free contact and communication with the outside world? May they

*Joel A. MacCallam has written an excellent book about cults, *Carnival of Souls,* in which he outlines the traits presented here.

read newspapers and books of their own choosing? May a group member read any translation of the Bible he chooses?

Theology: Does the group claim to be Christian, yet deny the deity of Christ? Does the leader claim deity? Does the group say that it recognizes the Bible as inspired, yet ignore or abuse large amounts of Scripture?

Deception: Are members encouraged to use deception to obtain their ends? Is any lie considered justifiable in order to gain converts and/or further the growth of the group?

Anti-Semitism: Does the group express an overt or covert hatred of Jews?

Selling salvation: Is the ability to give money to the group a requirement for obtaining favor with God? Is there a price placed on every activity?

Legitimate groups sometimes employ practices which are also characteristic of cults; this is what makes discernment so difficult. But if you are confronted by a group which uses many of the above techniques, you should clearly be on your guard.

College is a time to seek truth, to explore alternate patterns of thought, to establish one's own value system, to find direction for the future. This warning against cult involvement is not designed to hinder any of these desirable processes. But you should know that there are groups around whose goal is to exercise power over and extract money from unsuspecting individuals who trust blindly. Many cults are absolutely ruthless in their motives and methods of obtaining money and converts; sometimes their inductees do not even know that they are involved with a religious group until it is too late—the true nature of the group is not revealed until the inductee is emotionally, psychologically and socially crippled to the point that he cannot leave.

If you think that a group you are involved with seems suspicious, exercise extreme caution. Make no commitments; continue to question their practices; ask others on campus about the organization; contact campus chaplains or your church pastor and ask about the group. If this sort of careful examination on your part draws fire from the other members, you should be even *more* circumspect in your involvement.

DANGER ZONES

GAINING AN EDUCATION WITHOUT LOSING YOUR FAITH

To a Christian, college can be a dangerous place. Dangerous to faith, that is. The college years are years of seeking and questioning, of discovering new ideas and rubbing shoulders with life-styles and beliefs vastly different than ever before encountered. It is a time when all traditional values are held up for question and examination, a time of sifting and sorting; a time of wrestling for answers to spiritual questions.

How are you going to get through? You entered college with Christian faith. How will you leave? To a large extent, it could depend on what kind of school you are attending.

Dangers of the Secular Campus

The intellectual atmosphere on a secular campus will reflect the vast diversity of ideas in the world at large. University campuses are idea mills where concepts and theories are torn to shreds and examined for traces of truth. This questioning climate makes it difficult for preconceived ideas and casually accepted or shallow beliefs to flourish untouched. On a secular campus *all* ideas are inspected, digested, tested and molested; any dogmatically held beliefs are targeted as suspect and the person holding them is labeled unreasonable, boorish and thickheaded.

If you came to the university with just such unquestioned beliefs, you should prepare for confrontation now. It is not possible to avoid it, nor should you try. Remember this: truth will stand the test. If something you believe is valid, it can be questioned and studied and probed and it will come through. Do not be afraid to reevaluate your Christian beliefs. You may end up conceding some minor points and adding new flourishes to your theology, but the major tenets of your faith will stand the test.

The main agents of doubt will be your professors and your peers. There is a natural inclination on the part of students to emulate, imitate or even worship certain professors. The better profs understand this tendency and will not abuse their prestige with the students. But some are more than willing to exploit their position to influence students with their own personal prejudices. In such a case you might find a math professor who rails on and on about the abortion controversy and fully expects her students to trust her opinion on right-to-life as much as they trust her opinion about algebraic postulates.

When I was a freshman at Kearney State College, I needed to

take a certain sociology class for my major requirements. The class was taught by a young, popular professor and it was filled. I had to go through all sorts of bureaucratic gymnastics to get into the class, but finally was admitted. I went to my seat the first day of class feeling lucky—honored!—to have gotten into Prof. X's class.

He approached the podium in the lecture hall a few minutes late and called the class to attention. Before he handed out the syllabus, before he reviewed the grading system, before he took attendance, he began ranting about how religion—more specifically, Christianity—was the single greatest offender against social progress. He covered the Spanish Inquisition, the Crusades and Sunday "Blue Laws." He deplored the Puritans and their ethics; he exposed the church for its approval of slavery in the South; he cited Manifest Destiny as the doctrine which caused the demise of the American Indian. He stated simply that he would not put up with any nonsense from us, the students, when it came to religion. He then pulled a Bible from his briefcase and proceeded to tear out its pages and throw them in the air. When he was done, he hurled the spine of the book to the back of the lecture hall where I was sitting. Suitably satisfied with the shock value of his performance, he dismissed class.

Looking back on that experience, it is clear to me that the guy was a self-absorbed bigot. But I didn't see it so plainly at the time. My hard work at getting into the class, my need for the course to pursue my major, his personal aura, all confused the issue for me. I found his tirade offensive, but who was right? Well, he was partly right— that was the hard part. The church and Christians have to take responsibility for much of the wrongdoing in the world.

I was all alone when I had to decide whether or not I would stay in the class. Finally I decided to drop it and accept the consequences. My feeling was that, under the circumstances, it would be almost impossible for me to learn anything from the class, that he had antagonized me to the point that I would be unable to separate his valid teaching from his personal vendetta against religion. I had to go to his office and get his signature on my drop form, and I am sure that he snickered at me as I explained why I was dropping, especially since he had heard my pleas to get into the class only two days before.

You may have professors who abuse their position in more subtle ways. Still, it will be up to you to discern. Keep your strongest values and don't let yourself be taken advantage of unfairly. If a professor insists on playing on your inexperience and naivete, my suggestion is to find someone else who is more sympathetic toward your beliefs.

Actually, the really bad apples are rare. Secular schools hire their instructors from the ranks of society where both Christians and non-Christians abound. You are as likely to get a Christian professor at a secular school as not. There are many fine Christian people teaching and administering on secular campuses; they may not be immediately visible but they are there. When you find one, it's a great experience, because these are people who have integrated faith and learning at the highest level and are wonderful examples of how a Christian can operate in the world.

When it comes to your peers, the people you choose to be with, remember just that—you *choose* to be with them. There are all kinds of people in the student body at a large university. You are responsible for finding friends who will be supportive of your faith. They may not carbon-copy your beliefs but they should be sympathetic to your needs. In the dormitory or in the fraternity house you may have to look a long time before you find a "soul mate." Don't be discouraged. There are many organizations on campus with the express purpose of helping you get through college with a strong faith. Hook up with one of these groups (see p. 182).

"God may be subtle, but he isn't mean."

Albert Einstein

This is not to say that you should (or even can) isolate yourself from non-Christians. You need to be exposed to different types of people and different opinions. It's what you go to college for. A healthy mix of Christian and non-Christian associations will help you emerge from your experience at a secular university with a faith that has grown and matured.

Dangers of the Christian Campus

If the dangers on a secular campus are more direct, the dangers on a Christian campus are more devastating. More devastating because they are more subtle, more insidious. Kids attend Christian colleges because they want academic training that harmonizes with their faith. They want the close affinity of learning and fellowship with others of like mind and spirit and they expect it. This expectation is itself a danger.

The glossy brochures put out by the admissions office paint the campus as forty acres of heaven on earth. Inevitably, however, it cannot live up to its image because it is, after all, an institution, and institutions are nothing but collections of human beings— imperfect human beings. The clash of this harsh reality with the expectation of paradise on the part of the student can deal a staggering blow to faith.

Kirk Farnsworth, Professor of Psychology at Trinity College in Deerfield, Illinois, knows. "When students learn something in the classroom and see the opposite happening elsewhere in the institution, integration of faith and learning is destroyed!

"What we teach and how we

teach sets the tone for everything else that happens on campus—at least in the student's eyes. So, when students learn a Christian approach to business, leadership and the use of resources, for example, and see the opposite happening in Business Office policies, the leadership style of a dean or the president and the daily practices of the Food Service, it creates a tension that tears at the heart of the institution." And it tears at the heart of faith.

The discovery of diversity also strikes at the heart of faith. On a Christian campus you will find as much diversity of opinion and belief as on any secular campus, only it will be over matters of faith. To one who is suddenly confronted with differences in religious practices, tolerance, freedom and expression, the result can be disorienting and threatening. The realization that your fellow-students and instructors disagree with you, argue with you, or criticize you for your positions on doctrinal issues can be extremely upsetting.

The best defense against disillusionment is a change in expectations. Do not go to a Christian school expecting the answer to all of life's questions. Do not expect your weakness to vanish in the strength of others. Do not expect the institution, the faculty or the students to be infallible. This is unfair. Expect to be involved in a learning experience with other people of faith who are searching for answers to their questions, who are reaching out for support and encouragement. Expect to be challenged to greater patience and

understanding. Expect to examine what you believe in the light of new information.

> ## "There lives more faith in honest doubt, believe me, than in half the creeds."
>
> Tennyson

There is an additional danger present on the Christian college campus. The routine expression of faith—mandatory chapel services, classroom prayers, required Bible study, and religion classes—can become deadly ritual.

What was once done spontaneously on your own initiative is now a requirement in order to stay in good standing with an institution. This can take a previously meaningful experience and reduce it to a chore; it can dull the sharpest desire, quench even the most ardent spirit. If you find yourself day after day going through the motions and no longer attaching any particular significance to them, or just doing them because you must, faith can wither or become stagnant.

Try to understand the meaning behind the ritual. Mandatory chapel is meant to keep you from getting so involved in academic activities that you have no time for worship and spiritual instruction. As you walk into the service, prepare yourself to receive what is being offered. Put your other responsibilities and cares out of your mind and focus on God and what he wants you to do. Your chapel services may be anything but inspiring—a meaningless string of special speakers, panel discussions or announcements—but this time can still be used to present yourself to God in a special way as a student, a learner.

Another defense against the emptiness of such things as mandatory devotions or Bible reading is to go it one better—do *more* than is required. If students are expected to spend from 7:00 to 7:30 in Bible study and prayer each morning, get up early and spend from 6:30 to 7:30 on your devotions. Take a Bible class that is not required; ask a favorite professor to lead a discussion group on biblical perspectives applied to current social issues. This gives the initiative back to you—now you are doing it because *you* want to do it.

Perhaps the greatest threat to faith which is present at a Christian college is that eventually you will leave; the tight, close-knit fellowship of a religious institution delays the inevitable—integration into the "real" world. Sooner or later you must reconcile yourself to the fact that you will be living your life in secular society with non-Christians. True, some children are raised in Christian homes, attend Christian elementary and high schools, go to a Christian college, and are employed by a Christian organization; then they have children who attend Christian schools, and so on. But for most of us, the time eventually comes when we leave the safety, security and encouragement of the fold and are thrust into a job or other relationship with the secular world. Christian colleges sometimes fail to prepare for the jolt. Their graduates lose faith when they are no longer protected by their totally Christian environment. Lacking true maturity and needed coping skills, they flunk out of life. At one Bible college which prohibits unchaperoned dating and has very strict rules designed to keep males and females at a safe distance, the graduates tend to get married right after commencement—within weeks. The divorce rate among these graduates is almost 50 percent after only one year of marriage. Needless to say, this school does a great disservice to its students by failing to adequately prepare them for life in the real world.

> **"A young man who wishes to remain a sound atheist cannot be too careful of his reading. God is, if I may say it, very unscrupulous."**
>
> C. S. Lewis

If you are attending college in what you think is a sheltered environment, I can give no better advice than to periodically get outside that environment (in a manner acceptable to the administration). You will have to take a risk; you may face disappointment and discouragement. Maybe you need to tutor retarded children, or maybe you need to do volunteer work at the City Mission, or maybe you should *try* to get assigned to an inner-city school for your student teaching, or work with the elderly in your area, or do visitation at the jail. Any of these would provide you with the needed dose of *reality* which is missing.

A friend of mine attended a conservative Bible school in Chicago. During her first year there she wrote to me that a requirement of the school was that she do street evangelism in a very rough part of town with another girl. As they walked to their assigned area they passed through a dangerous neighborhood; to protect themselves against molesters, they held hands and cuddled each other when they walked down the street, pretending to be lesbians so that no one would bother them.

As I read her letter—myself a student at a large state school—I wondered who was leading the sheltered life! Before, I would have said that it was her, because she went to a "fundie" Bible school where she couldn't wear short dresses, couldn't date and couldn't wear makeup. In spite of those facets of the school's policy, she was bridging the gap between the hothouse environment of her Christian community and the "way of the world." I did not encounter that type of challenge at a secular school.

There is no perfect atmosphere for learning—not for a Christian, especially. There will always be conflicts, disappointments, challenges and direct threats to the faith of a student who is committed to Christ. You will change your mind about certain things while you are in college—that's good! That's what you want! If you don't grow, your money and time will have been wasted. You will question previous beliefs; some will be discarded and others will be embraced more fervently.

Whether you go to a Christian school or a secular university, you will face dangers to your faith and belief. Do not panic, do not be afraid. Analyze what the threat is and try to get the help you need to see you through. The encouragement of other Christians will probably be your most valuable resource during this time.

In the final analysis, *you* will be responsible for the growth or demise of your faith. Don't blame your confusion on the amorality of your college roommate or the hypocrisy of the religion professor. The school you are attending is an introduction to a broader world-view and now is as good a time as any to face life as it is. You can come out of school with a system of belief which has been fed and nurtured, pruned and trimmed, stronger in every way. It's up to you.

Living Spaces 11

THE
WELL-APPOINTED
DORM ROOM

1. *Linens*—If sheets, towels and bedspreads are not provided by the residence hall, or if the additional fee charged for linen service is high, you will be bringing your own linens to school. We suggest that you buy towels and sheets which you will be able to distinguish from those of others. Pick blankets and a bedspread that will stand up to all the kids who will be sitting and/or walking on them.

2. *Lamp*—For studying late into the night, keeping peace with your roommate and on friendly terms with your baby-blues, nothing beats a high-intensity lamp.

3. *Computer, word processor, or typewriter*—Even if you plan on having all your papers typed by a professional, you may get into a pinch and have to pound out your own work.

4. *Clock*—Bring an electric or battery-run alarm clock to school with you, so as not to miss those important classes, tests and dates. Do not trust your reputation for punctuality to a wind-up type clock, which will invariably let you down. Along these same lines . . .

5. *Calendar*—Before you leave home, try to find out when family members have their birthdays, anniversaries, etc. Mark those important dates on a calendar, and refer to it once in a while, taking appropriate action; you know, a card, a gift, flowers. A wall calendar with enough space for writing the important daily events such as tests, term paper due dates, etc. will be a valuable tool in organizing your time.

6. *Posters*—There's nothing like a poster or two to provide inexpensive decoration for your drab little cell. A picture of Uncle Sam and his pointed finger will often give students (especially male students) added incentive . . .

7. *Laundry stuff*—Bring a laundry basket, detergent, hangers, and rolls of change for the washers and dryers. Depending on your wardrobe or dorm facilities, consider packing an iron.

8. *Entertainment*—Before you bring your 23" color console with the VCR or your 600-watt stereo system, 1) check with your roommate to see what he or she is bringing; 2) consider the size of your speakers in relation to the size of your dorm room; 3) find out the rules about playing music—when and how loud; and 4) determine the security of your equipment.

9. *Popcorn popper, hot pot, and small refrigerator*—The popper may not be necessary; many dorms have lounges or kitchenettes with microwave ovens for residents' use. The hot pot is essential for heating water, soup, etc. If allowed, and if you can afford it, a small-sized frig can be a useful item.

10. *Dishes*—At the very least you will need a plate, bowl, knife-fork-spoon, medium-sized cutting knife, large serving spoon, large serving bowl, hot drink mug, drinking glass, can opener. Those are the essentials.

11. *Food*—You will want to keep the following staples on hand:
   —popcorn, oil, salt or microwave popcorn
   —hot and cold drink mixes
   —crackers, cookies
   —peanut butter, jelly
   —canned soup, spaghetti, hash, etc.

Such a cache will preserve you from hunger during study marathons, all-night philosophy discussions and missed meals at the cafeteria.

12. *Mouse trap*—Actually, you don't want to have to place traps around your room—too dangerous for bare feet. So be sure that you have put all your foodstuffs in airtight containers or in the dorm refrigerator, so as to avoid sharing your room with rodents and roaches. If your carelessness draws critters, you will be very unpopular with the other residents.

13. *Miscellaneous*—Consider the following: a small bucket for shower supplies, case for toiletries, deck of cards, extension cords, and sewing supplies.

GROOMING A ROOMIE

Whether you live on campus in a dormitory, in your sorority or fraternity house or off campus in an apartment with five other guys, you're probably going to have a roommate during most of your college life. Maybe you will be able to choose who you share your quarters with and maybe you won't. If you do get to choose, you may be surprised later with what you got. Consider these suggestions for getting along with, yea, even enjoying your college roommate.

Go into it with a realistic attitude. Resign yourself to the fact that concessions will have to be made.

Nothing goes without saying. Talk about everything that is important to you. Your mutual need for privacy in the midst of lack of space and personal room must be communicated. Explain why you need to have a corner to yourself or your own shelf in the bathroom. Explain why you need to speak on the telephone privately at times, and why you must have a quiet time every

morning before breakfast. Only the biggest jerk will infringe when you have given the "why" of your request.

From the beginning, try to reach an agreement with your roomie about these things:

- —playing music: type, volume, hours.
- —housekeeping: standards to be maintained, possible division of labor to see that it's taken care of.
- —shared expenses: laundry charges, cleaning supplies, decorating, food, utilities.
- —telephone: cost and use.
- —visiting hours: when they are, who is invited, communication techniques on when to stay away or get out.
- —smoking and/or drinking in the room.
- —contraband: the best advice here is that you each respect each other's rights by agreeing not to have anything illegal or administration-forbidden in the room.

—hours: reconciling the early bird and the night owl.
—space: closet, study, personal.
—borrowing: clothes, books, personal property.

Take it slow in your relationship. Ideally you want to have a roommate who is a good listener, close friend, an "A" student and a sensitive comrade. If you rush toward such a relationship you may lose all chance of achieving it. It is also possible to have a wonderful roommate who is none of these things. You will be living together for a least a semester, so don't push things; just let the relationship develop at its own pace.

"Everybody thinks of changing humanity and nobody thinks of changing himself."

Count Leo Tolstoy

Of the two (or three or seven) people involved, *you* are going to be the easiest one to change. In the final analysis, it is *you* who has the greatest control over the situation through your willingness to cooperate and compromise.

Don't take advantage of your roommate. Don't expect her to lie for you, lend you her clothes, do your assignments for you or stay out of the room indefinitely while you entertain your boyfriend. Some aim-to-please people will let you get away with this sort of thing in order to make a friend, but it's not fair and in the end it will backfire in hurt feelings. And don't do these things for someone else. Your relationship must be based on mutual respect.

If it isn't working out and you've talked to your roommate about your gripes, then the next person to see is the Resident Advisor or Student Assistant on your floor (if you're in a dorm) or the Housemother (if you're in a fraternity or sorority). It will help if you have worked out a possible solution beforehand—such as switching roommates with two other people who aren't getting along either. If you are living off campus in an apartment, you have a bigger problem. You have a lease, probably, and limited options as to what you can feasibly do. As a general rule, the person who moves out should still be financially responsible to hold up his end until another roommate can be found to take his place. He may be legally obligated to do so, too.

Living with a previously total stranger is an adventure where the outcome is largely up to you. You may find that in the course of your college life you never get any satisfaction from the arrangement. On the other hand, you may make a friend who becomes a lifetime confidant and companion.

APARTMENT FOR RENT

The way some people talk, you'd think the first goal of any self-respecting student is to find an apartment off campus. It is, after all, the thing to do—it's grown up, it's chic, it's your badge of freedom. It is the Declaration of Independence.

Depending on the college you attend, however, there is probably a time-honored rule of "on-campus residence." Usually, students are required to spend at least their first year in a dorm—unless they have a very good reason why not, such as living at home, being married or having part-time commuter status.

Some colleges require the majority of their students to live on campus the majority of the time—all four years, in some cases. And in other colleges, because of location, say, it's just easier to live on campus than off.

Be that as it may, the idea of moving out of the dorm is going to occur to you sometime in your college career. Somewhere between the time your infatuation with the residence hall wears off (during the first week) and the time you walk down the aisle for your sheepskin, you're going to consider finding your own digs.

Before you get all your earthly possessions tied up in bundles and ready to move, there are a few facts you ought to consider:

ROOMS FOR RENT
611-3416
• AT THE COTTAGE TOWERS, WEST HILL. •

Fact #1—Finding the right apartment is hard work. It's not just a matter of packing up and moving in; there are a jillion details to be considered, most of them having to do with the lease. See, in most college towns, renting apartments to students is big business. The landlords see you not as a fresh-faced, earnest student but as an ambulatory gold mine. It's their game and they write the rules—fix the rental price, decide what you can or cannot do on the premises, enforce the terms of the lease, etc.

If you think that you'll just rent any old apartment you happen to come across, be warned. With that attitude you're a plum ripe for the picking. Finding the right apartment—that is, one that has a good location, a fair rental rate, a conscientious landlord and all the amenities of home—will take a determined effort on your part.

Fact #2—You're at a disadvantage. The whole process is designed to favor the landlord and protect his interests, not yours. You have some rights, to be sure. Do you know what they are? If not, get in touch with the school's housing office. They'll have information regarding your rights as a tenant. Or contact a local legal advocacy program—they'll set you straight.

Fact #3—It is expensive, and unless you plan on taking in a roommate or two, it may be beyond your reach. Landlords know that college students share rent and living expenses as a matter of course; so they charge the highest rent the market will allow. You can bargain with them, of course, and try to get the price down but in most cases it's a futile effort. They don't have to rent to you because the next guy will take it, no questions asked.

Fact #4—You'll be

removed from campus activities. After the euphoria of setting up housekeeping evaporates, you just might feel yourself a trifle out of things. Your focus will not be the campus anymore; it will be the apartment. You'll find yourself losing contact with campus happenings—which means you'll have to spend a greater amount of time and effort just keeping up with what's going on. That is, if you *want* to keep up. For some, it's not a bad thing to remove themselves from the campus; it cuts out a lot of Mickey Mouse rigamarole and allows greater concentration on important things like studies.

Fact #5—An

apartment won't solve all your problems. At first blush the idea of an apartment sounds like an oasis in the barrens of academia. Unfortunately, renting your own place creates as many or more problems than it solves living-wise. If you think dorm codes are restrictive, wait until you read a lease! If you think roommates are a hassle, wait until your apartment-mate uses up all the hot water and won't pay her half of the rent when it's due. If you think studying in the dorm is tough, wait until you have a test to cram for and the folks in 3B (also students) decide to party until 3 A.M.

Fact #6—Maintaining

an apartment is hard work. As if school was not enough, now you have to clean the oven and defrost the freezer on your off-hours, too. What's more, you get to pay for the privilege. Apartments take a lot more upkeep than dorm rooms— more area to clean, more appliances to malfunction, more hassles all around. At least at the dorm you didn't have to carry the garbage to the curb, scour the communal shower or clean the stove top.

If, after considering the facts of apartment life, you still believe an off-campus move to be the best thing for you, you'll need all the help you can get to find a good apartment . . . one just right for you.

Newspapers—both the campus and local town newspaper—will have ads for apartments. Consult them daily; it will give you a good idea of what the rental market is like.

Many retail stores—cafes, record stores, supermarkets—have bulletin boards that people use to pass on the word about good available living space. Check them out, and let the store manager know you're looking and ask him to have any likely prospects give you a call if anything turns up.

The Student Housing Office on campus can give you leads for off-campus living. Landlords who *want* to rent to students keep in touch with the housing office. Furthermore, the school is likely to have the scoop on unscrupulous rent-rats you'll want to avoid.

Talk to people. You never know who will pop up with the prize you're after. Many of the best apartment deals are never advertised formally. Word of mouth is all that's needed. Tell *everyone* you meet—classmates, friends, instructors, waitresses, gas station attendants—that you're apartment hunting. Chances are, even if they don't know of anything specific, they'll know someone else you can ask.

Comb the neighborhoods you would like to live in, searching for rental signs. Stop at likely places and ask about apartments in the neighborhood. People with large homes near campuses rent out rooms in upper floors. The homeowners in the neighborhood know where these houses are.

Expand your idea of an apartment. Suitable living space need not be an eightplex, or a multilevel apartment house. It can be a single large bedroom in a family home. Many wonderful arrangements involve students living with a local family— sometimes even rent-free in consideration of other services: companionship to an elderly person, child care, maintenance around the house, etc. You could luck out and find yourself not only with a great apartment, but free meals and a second family too.

Always inspect the apartment carefully. You want to make a good impression on the landlord the same way you would in a job interview. At the same time, you want to see what you're getting for your money and develop a sense of comparison for later bargaining. If you think the rent is too high for a basement space with only six-foot ceilings, you want to be able to tell the landlord that the place down the street has eight-foot ceilings and is thirty dollars cheaper! This sort of information is invaluable in the marketplace.

Ask questions. The time to find out about the "little details" is before you are serious about renting. Satisfy yourself on every point. Find out if you can have a roommate, if you have a nine-month or a twelve-month lease, if utilities are included, if you can sublet, if you can use the garage or storage space in the attic, what furniture stays, whether the landlord has the right to enter your apartment—whatever you wonder about, ask.

Never sign anything without reading it carefully. Whether you sign a "standard" form-printed lease or a simple letter of agreement, be certain you read and comprehend what you are signing. If you can't understand it, get help, or get a lawyer to look it over for you. It is, after all, a legally binding document. Go over the lease with the landlord; ask about all the items you don't understand. If you don't like certain things—that the landlord requires a $250 pet deposit for your canary—get them changed in the lease before you sign it. If you want something spelled out that isn't in the document—that the landlord cannot enter your apartment without your permission—get it included. An unsigned lease is not unchangeable. You can make it fit your situation, no matter what any previous tenants may have signed. If you can't reach agreement on points that are important to you, go elsewhere.

DORM LIFE DREARY? THEN BUY A CONDO

Remember college housing—the old cinderblock dorm rooms and the off-campus pads furnished in Early Salvation Army? Well, all that has changed, at least for an affluent few at the University of Texas at Austin. About 500 UT students have become condominium dwellers, enjoying fireplaces, swimming pools, microwave ovens and jacuzzis. The money, of course, comes from their parents, who have more in mind than spoiling the kids: condominiums have been good investments. Some realtors claim that they are appreciating as much as 35 percent a year, and developers like Charles Marsh "are buying up every scrap of land within reach of the campus."

Student condomania has struck a few other parts of the country as well; but Texas, where a lot of wealthy people

don't have to spend much on tuition, is a natural. Les Hughes, a Conroe, Texas apartment developer, bought one for $57,000 three years ago for a daughter who just graduated. Another daughter is about to move in, and the way prices are going, the value will have doubled by the time she graduates. More enterprising is Julie Roush, a junior who bought her own condo with down-payment money she earned working part-time. Her father pays the mortgage and she will get the proceeds. Even middle-class parents have figured out that they might as well be paying a mortgage, getting a tax break, and waiting for a resale profit instead of spending up to $4,000 a year on a dormitory room. One Austin real-estate firm now caters almost exclusively to the student market. Its ads read, "A condo for you. A tax write-off for Dad."

from Newsweek,
January 25, 1982

205

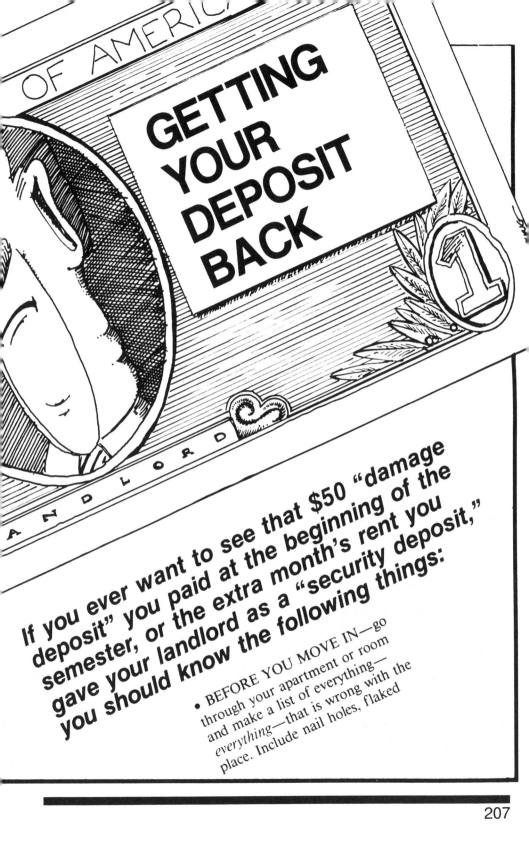

GETTING YOUR DEPOSIT BACK

If you ever want to see that $50 "damage deposit" you paid at the beginning of the semester, or the extra month's rent you gave your landlord as a "security deposit," you should know the following things:

- BEFORE YOU MOVE IN—go through your apartment or room and make a list of everything—*everything*—that is wrong with the place. Include nail holes, flaked paint, chipped porcelain, damaged linoleum, holes or stains in the carpet, missing brackets on the curtain rods, broken or cracked light fixtures, damage to the furniture. Check out the appliances: Are the drip pans on the stove clean? Is there a broiler pan in the oven? A butter dish in the refrigerator? How many, if any, ice cube trays are in the freezer? Are there light bulbs in the oven, refrigerator and all other appliances and fixtures? You may find that when you move out you will be charged for the replacement of things that never existed if you don't make a note of it now. Present your list to your landlord or the maintenance staff in the dorm. This has a two-fold purpose: first, you want them to repair or replace defective items. Second, you have protected yourself against later accusations that *you* cracked the glass top of the coffee table or stained the toilet bowl. Have your landlord sign the list and keep a copy. Do this no later than one week after you move in.

> ## Keep cleaning supplies organized and portable by putting them in a six-liter soft drink carton.

• WHILE YOU ARE THERE— *think* before you do anything to the room; think how it will look when you move out. You will have to make good on every nail hole in the wall. Don't hang big heavy objects that might cause damage. Don't put anything up with that adhesive putty because it 1) doesn't work and 2) leaves a greasy stain on the wall.

You won't want to spend all your time cleaning, granted; but you'll be thankful later if you do a few routine things. Keep the bathroom tub, sink and stool clean since rust stains and mineral deposits that build up over time are very hard to remove. Use an in-tank toilet bowl cleaner if you're not inclined to scrub. You can keep most grit off the tub and sink by wiping occasionally with an old nylon stocking. If you have carpet, vacuum it once in a while. If you are really opposed to this sort of thing, and you have enough money to swing it (or enough roommates to pitch in), you might consider having a housekeeper come in every week; sometimes other students hire out as "domestics," and near large campuses there are housecleaning services you can employ.

If something major goes wrong, contact maintenance or your landlord immediately. For example, a slow-draining sink might be a simple thing to fix now and a major repair—for which you will be charged—later on.
• WHEN YOU MOVE OUT—it's best to remove your belongings from the apartment or room and then tackle the cleaning and repairs. You will be expected to leave it in its original good(?) condition. If the place was filthy when you arrived

and your landlord understands that you know it was filthy, then leave it the way you found it. You will be expected to have the oven clean, refrigerator wiped out, sinks scoured, floors swept and mopped, carpet vacuumed, furniture dusted. You usually don't have to wax floors, shampoo carpet, clean windows or polish woodwork (as though you were even *considering* doing all that).

> **Put a big piece of aluminium foil in the bottom of the oven so spills don't land on the metal, which is much harder to clean than aluminium foil is to replace.**

You can easily spackle nail holes by mixing toothpaste (no stripes or gels, please) with crushed aspirin and filling the hole with the goo. Just use your fingers. If the walls are colored, you can tint your toothpaste/spackle with make-up.

Now get your landlord, or whoever is in charge, to inspect the apartment with you. If you just skip town, you will never see your deposit. If you are living on campus, you can be reasonably assured that your efforts at keeping your room nice will be rewarded. If you are living off campus in a college town, you should realize that you may have a landlord who

has *never* returned a deposit. He has targeted students for the old security deposit rip-off. He may have a point—most students don't deserve to have their money back. But if you do, tell him. Any unjust refusal on his part can be dealt with legally, but perhaps the threat of a phone call to the city housing authority or campus housing office is all you would need.

Get out your list of things that were initially wrong and go through your room or apartment with the S.A. or landlord. You are allowed normal wear-and-tear. That means that if you've been living in the apartment for nine months and consequently the hallway carpeting isn't as nice and fluffy as it was when you moved in, it's nothing you should have to pay for. Things like carpet wear out eventually. If the landlord says he's going to keep, say, a dollar back for every light bulb that is missing, tell him you'll go and replace them yourself, because you can do it for less than that. It is not unusual for them to charge $5 for each dirty drip pan on the stove (which cost $1.79 at K-Mart and which they will not replace for the next tenant) or $2 for a refrigerator butter tray (which was lost eight years ago) or $25 for "cleaning" (which you have already done and they will not do again).

When everything checks out, get your money then and there—it's yours. In some states, landlords have to return your money with interest. If your school levied a deposit, they will almost never refund it to you before you leave— look for a check in the mail.

LEADER OF THE LAUNDROMAT

One of these days you're going to have to do your laundry. Up until now you have taken enough weekend trips home or paid your roommate or simply done without clean socks. Eventually, even you will begin to consider a change of underwear, and that means washing clothes.

Where to Go

If you live in a dorm, there are probably washers and dryers on your floor or in the basement; if you are in a big apartment building, there are machines on the premises. They may be the closest thing but far from the best thing. Check into commercial laundromats which may be cheaper or more efficient. They often have enough machines so that you can do one or two weeks' laundry all at once, large folding tables and racks to hang up permanent press clothes. (And remember that good things can happen at the laundromat—Carl Dean met Dolly Parton at a Wishee-Washee in Nashville. They got married and lived happily ever after.)

What to Bring

1. Your dirty clothes in laundry baskets or sturdy corrugated cardboard boxes. Duffle bags don't work well once your clothes are clean and folded.

2. Clothes hangers.
3. Detergent. Don't buy it at the laundromat—those little boxes are cute but expensive. Get a good supply at a supermarket (cheaper than the campus bookstore). Your best bet is a liquid detergent with fabric softener added. These are easy to lug around and less expensive than buying both detergent and fabric softener.
4. Measuring cup.

What to Do

1. Sort your clothes, segregating light colors from dark and sturdy fabrics from delicates. It only takes one "Go Big Red" sweatshirt tossed in with the whites to make you the laughingstock of the locker room. A new pair of jeans has a similar effect. There are tags inside your clothes which warn you of such pitfalls—read them. They will tell you if it is safe to wash in warm

water, if the garment can be put in the dryer and if it's likely to bleed. If if says to wash dark colors separately, don't be adventuresome. The tag people *know* of what they speak.

2. Read the directions for the washers. They are printed inside the lid or posted on the wall. Measure your detergent, put it in the machine and turn it on. Add your clothes. Fill to the top of the machine, but don't tamp the stuff down. Try to distribute the weight of the clothes evenly, or the machine will tilt during the spin cycle.

3. While the clothes are washing, do any hand laundry you may have in the big tubs provided. Use the same detergent as you would for your regular wash unless the label recommends something else, like Woolite.

4. Now your clothes are washed. Remember this: *washing machines eat clothes.* Make sure you get every last sock and bandanna out of the machine. Another bit of sage wisdom: *dryers melt clothes.* Commercial dryers inevitably have two settings: air dry (no heat) and fire dry. Be forewarned. The dryers are usually big and can handle two or more washer loads at a time, but if you fill them too full you'll waste your dimes. Check the progress of your clothes from

time to time, making especially certain that your polyesters aren't melting.

5. As soon as they are dry, put the clothes you want unwrinkled on hangers; shirts and slacks should never be put back into the laundry basket. Fold the other clothes promptly—it'll save time later. You don't want to iron.

Four more pieces of advice:

1. Save badly stained clothes for Christmas vacation. Your mom knows what to do.

2. If you washed a garment according to the instructions on the label and it got ruined, return it. If the red trim on your white shirt turns the fabric around it pink, that's not your fault and you should get your money back. (As a rule, save all sales tags and receipts until the garment has been washed once.)

3. Remember the old combat movies where the general pressed his pants by putting them between the mattress and box spring of his bed at night while he slept on it? That works.

4. Crowded·closets cause wrinkled clothes. If at all possible, give your clothes room to breathe and they'll look nice when it's time to wear them. When confronted with a wrinkled dress or shirt before a school banquet, take your shower with the article of clothing hanging on the shower rod; the steam created in the bathroom will remove the wrinkles

COMBATING COMMUTER ANGST

• Kirk grew up in Oakdale and wanted to attend the state college there. To save money he decided to live at home; that way he wouldn't have to get a job to pay for the room and board at the dorm, giving him more time to concentrate on academics.

• Janelle got married the summer after she graduated from high school and now, three years later, was going to start her college education. She and her husband lived about a mile and a half from the campus of the small, private college she attended.

• Sarah did not like living in the dorm. Although it was mandatory for single, full-time students to live in a residence hall for the first two years, as soon as she had enough hours to make her a junior she and two friends moved off campus into the upstairs of an old house.

• Dan was a psychology major who managed to land a job in a children's home for predelinquent and emotionally disturbed boys. One of the benefits of the job was that it provided room and board along with a small salary in exchange for his counseling services.

All of these students were lucky to have the living arrangements they did. But they found themselves missing out on important aspects of college life because they were commuting students. While other kids were enjoying the camaraderie and activities that go with living on campus, they were driving back and forth, juggling nonschool commitments, wandering around campus with an armload of books and lab equipment and generally feeling out of it. Even students who don't think they'll miss campus life, like Sarah, invariably discover that they are out of sync with school activities and that staying on top of it academically becomes harder and harder.

Unless you attend a junior college or other school which has no on-campus living facilities, your school is geared toward the kid who lives on campus. For example, there are no towels in the locker room after gym class because everyone just goes back to the dorm to shower; there are no classes from 11:30 to 12:30 because that's when the dining hall is open; there are no lockers, because the on-campus students keep all their extra books and supplies in their room; the instructors plan evening rap sessions and study seminars in the dorms; the library is closed over Thanksgiving and Christmas and Easter because nobody is on campus. And maybe you find it hard to meet people because they already have their social life which revolves around the dorm and aren't interested in making more friends. They don't know why you are in their class, if you're a full-time student or what. In fact, they don't give you a second thought.

A Place to Be

Your greatest problem as a commuting student is that during the course of the day you have no headquarters. You can't run back to your room to change into old clothes before your Art class. You must bring to school with you everything you will need for the day, and sometimes you'll forget things. If you drive to school you can use your car as a depository, but if you have to park eight blocks off campus or if you take the bus to school, even that is not available to you. Some colleges provide lockers for the use of commuting students, but not all.

The best thing to do is to find someone living on campus who will let you use her room. You can drop off your gym clothes there in the morning and (if you're good friends) nap there between classes. You can make a phone call there or eat your sack lunch in private.

If you can't find a student who is willing to share her room with you, ask one of your instructors if he'll let you leave your things in his office. This is sometimes even more convenient because his office is closer to your classes, although this arrangement does not give you the entrée into dorm life that you might prefer.

Do make an effort to find a comfortable place to hang out. Depending on your campus, it might take weeks to find the best lounges: the quiet ones, the social ones, the intimate cozy ones, the ones with televisions, the ones with tables, the ones where you can get some work done. When you pick one place to frequent, you will find there are others who are regulars, too, and eventually you can get to know them.

Taking the Offensive

To get into the swing you must stick your neck out. Try these strategies:

1. Eat breakfast or lunch in the cafeteria. Most schools will issue a meal ticket for just one meal a day, or you may pay on a meal-by-meal basis.

2. Between classes, go to the student union. Strike up a conversation with the people who are in your classes.

3. Make it a point to attend extracurricular activities on campus. Go to basketball games, track meets, school plays.

4. Join a club—either a special interest club or a study group. You will meet other students who share your interests.

5. Once you have met a few people, invite them to your digs. You will be amazed at how grateful they will be to get off campus. If you are living at home, you have a home-cooked meal to offer; if you have an apartment, they will appreciate the opportunity to go someplace where they can turn the stereo up and let their hair down. If you are married, you might like to double-date with another unmarried couple or have them over for dinner.

6. Take advantage of the "extras" that on-campus students take for granted. For example, you can use the campus gym and swimming pool in the evenings and you can get into the biology lab at night to work on your experiment and you can watch television in the dormitory lounge.

7. Try to land a job on campus. While it may not pay as well as a job in town, it will provide the opportunity to meet other students and keep in touch with campus goings-on.

8. In general, stay on campus as many hours per day as is feasible. Study in the library instead of at home; eat at the cafeteria instead of at McDonalds; go to the movie at the Union instead of the Bijou. It may be noisier, less appetizing or less entertaining, respectively, but you will be absorbing the atmosphere of the college and that is your goal.

Commuting has traditionally been viewed as a disadvantage for the college student. Most parents and staff believe that the greatest benefit is derived when a full-time student lives on campus, totally immersed in the ambiance of college life.

But as a commuting student, you have the opportunity to enjoy the best of two worlds. You are free of the protected, sometimes restrictive life that is led by students who live on campus and yet you can take advantage of the many social, recreational and academic programs offered by your school. You can decide to what extent you wish to take part in college life, choosing to participate in the helpful and declining the meaningless.

Outplacement 12

EIGHT REASONS TO CONSIDER
A TRANSFER

1. You cannot in any way afford the school you are attending.

2. You discover an area of interest that you want to pursue and another school has a better program in that area.

3. You are doing poorly academically, and you believe it is caused by some feature of the school (city campus, not enough individual attention from the faculty, learning environment too restrictive).

4. You want to go to a local (junior) college for your first two years but actually get your diploma from a more prestigious institution.

5. You want to vary your college experience.

6. You find yourself unable to adjust to proscriptions of the college (no drinking, no off-campus residence, etc.).

7. You are totally unhappy and genuinely feel that a change of scenery will solve the problem. For example, you are on a small campus where the presence of an ex-boyfriend is painful, you are too far away from your family and feel insecure, or you are in a big school and are unable to find your niche.

8. You qualify for a scholarship or other significant form of financial aid at another school and wish to take advantage of it.

WHEN FACING ACADEMIC DISMISSAL

1. Ask yourself, "Do I want another chance to make it at college?" Maybe so, maybe no. If you do . . .

2. See the professor(s) who gave the low marks and try to get them changed. Most will not want to be personally responsible for the demise of your college career.

3. Check the college catalog and any other relevant sources to make sure your dismissal was by the book. If not, it may be overturned.

4. Petition the correct college official and/or committee with a request for reinstatement. Often just this show of good faith will cause a change. State your intention of doing better; establish any extenuating circumstances which caused your low grades.

5. Appeal to a higher authority in the school—perhaps the vice-president or dean in charge of academic affairs. Many schools have a legal advocacy program which you can use (usually an upperclassman who can present your case).

6. Last resort: Consult an attorney and take the case to a civil court. This is costly, time-consuming and creates ill-will, but if you really feel you have not been treated fairly, that your dismissal is illegal and unjustified, it can be done.

Condensed from *The Other Way to Better Grades* by Marvin Karlins.

---

20 FAMOUS PEOPLE WHO NEVER ATTENDED COLLEGE

1. Joseph Chamberlain, British statesman
2. Grover Cleveland, U.S. President
3. Joseph Conrad, British author
4. Aaron Copland, U.S. composer
5. Hart Crane, U.S. poet
6. Eugene Debs, U.S. socialist leader
7. Amelia Earhart, U.S. aviator
8. Paul Gauguin, French painter
9. Khalil Gibran, Syrian author and painter
10. Ernest Hemingway, U.S. author
11. Rudyard Kipling, British author
12. Abraham Lincoln, U.S. President
13. H. L. Mencken, U.S. editor and journalist
14. John D. Rockefeller, U.S. oil magnate
15. Eleanor Roosevelt, U.S. lecturer, author, and humanitarian
16. George Bernard Shaw, British playwright and critic
17. Dylan Thomas, British poet
18. Harry S. Truman, U.S. President
19. George Washington, U.S. President
20. Virginia Woolf, British author

From *The Book of Lists*

CHOOSING A MAJOR, CHOOSING A CAREER

Doctor, lawyer, Indian chief. Microsurgeon, public defender, political campaign strategist. What do you want to be? Do you have a romantic ideal that you still cling to? Do you want to be a ballerina in the Joffrey? Are your parents concerned about your vocation? Does your father want you to get a degree in agronomy so you can come back and help run the farm? Your advisor can prove to you that your talent lies in the quantitative sciences on the basis of your test scores, so why do you still want to be a police officer? Since tenth grade you have seen yourself as an English professor, reading the classics over and over again, imparting your wisdom to impressionable minds. Where's the future in that?

How are you going to decide on a major, on a career? How are you going to decide on next semester's classes, or this semester's? Your degree of commitment or confusion makes you one of the following types:

Type A: You are

absolutely sure of your goal, and single-minded in its pursuit. You are also in the minority. You are most likely looking forward to a career in a profession for which you are uniquely qualified because of a certain talent, such as operatic singing or playing professional football. Or you plan to enter a field where preparation begins early on, such as medicine: you have taken a heavy science load since you were in junior high, worked as a nurse's aide after school since you were sixteen, and now it's time to take a solid pre-med course so you can get into a good medical school.

1. Define your goal specifically, research it and find out exactly what you need to get where you are going. Stay current in your information; the requirements of your chosen field may be very different now than when you first contemplated it.

2. Make sure you are attending a school that will help you get where you want to go. If you are planning on medical school, you should not attend a Bible college which has no science program unless you are willing to take supplemental classes at another school or after you graduate which will qualify you for med school. You can find out before you enter college how many of your school's alumni go on to graduate school, for example. This is a good indication of how well they are prepared for post-college training. You may find that you will have to transfer to another

college midway in your studies.

3. Reevaluate your decision at intervals. Not every day—just once in a while. Circumstances change. For example, you may want to be a lawyer so that you can work in public defense. But the funds for public defense lawyers have been cut back considerably. Besides that, there are virtually no openings. Keeping your primary objective in mind—helping the poor—you may wish to change your career to social work or church pastoring in an economically depressed area.

4. Force yourself to have some existence outside your career goal. You need to have extracurricular activities which are unrelated to your primary vocational interest. It's often a good idea to take elective courses in another field; this is to make you a more well-rounded person. You may also find a latent interest in some unexplored area which should be addressed before you commit heart and soul to your lifelong passion.

Type B: You have

absolutely no direction. You have no idea in the world what you are doing in college, or where you will go when you leave. You are a leaf in the wind, with no purpose to your present activity. You're in the minority too, although you have a bit more company than Type A who has no doubts whatsoever.

1. You have a lot of research to do. Perhaps you are undecided because you are uninformed. Just for fun, go to the library and get *The Dictionary of Occupational Titles.* This tome is put out by the U.S. Department of Labor and lists every job title there is. It will surprise you. Start scanning the lists and you'll find jobs that intrigue you. Now read *The Occupational Outlook Handbook* or the *Occupational Outlook for College Graduates* or some other book like that, also at the library. This will give you a general idea of what is hot and what is not as far as gaining employment is concerned.

Your research has shown you what the scope of the market is, and what's a good bet from a practical point of view. Now go to your advisor. Plead with her for help. Confess your indecision. This person is interested in keeping you in school; therefore she is interested in giving you a motivation for staying there (employment after graduation). She will be helpful.

2. Concentrate on your general distribution courses. Do as well as you can in all of them. You don't know now which ones might be in your major field later on. When you find a class which is especially to your liking, visit with the professor to see what related classes are available and what career might come out of your interest.

3. Don't take courses on a pass-fail basis at this point. If you decide to go into chemical engineering, you'll be sorry you took Organic Chemistry pass-fail because that means that it can't count toward your major hours requirement, and you're going to have to stay in school another semester to make it up.

4. You are a candidate for

"stopping out." It may take a semester or two or three in the real world for you to figure out what you want to study in college. You should consider accepting an internship or just getting a job to see how it feels.

5. If you are still undecided after all of this, you are probably tempted to drop out of school indefinitely. After all, it's costing everyone a lot of time and money to educate you, and you're not going to make good on that investment. This is a judgment call. There is definitely a value to education aside from career preparation. Many educators contend that the only true value of education is to prepare one for life, to create individuals who know how to think, who know how to learn and have an informed world-view from which to base future decisions. But others contend that college is a form of advanced technical training which is wasted on those who have your kind of problem—deciding what you are going to do with that training.

It's up to you. Continue to ask questions, evaluate your own interests and seek the advice of others.

Type C: You know

pretty much what you want to do, but are open to other ideas. You are in the majority. You came to college with an idea that you would major in psychology, but your roommate is majoring in recreation because she wants to work at a YMCA, and that sounds like a great job too.

1. Again, you must do your research. Research your target field of study and the other fields you are interested in. Make sure the courses being offered in your major area are generally appealing to you and that you are fairly sure you can get good grades in them. Go ahead and read the books recommended to the Type B who has no ideas.

2. Talk to the professionals in your field. The nursing classes you are taking are interesting, but you may find that burnout in the nursing professions is frighteningly common. Do you want to do that for the rest of your life? Ah, but you could become a nurse-midwife, and that's really exciting—everyone you talked to said so. Now you're getting somewhere.

You are taking psychology classes because you want to do counseling, but a marriage counselor in town says that it's next to impossible to establish any kind of practice without a Ph.D. Are you willing to go that far with your education? Try to extrapolate your decision into the years ahead and see if the major you have chosen will take you where you want to go.

3. Make your classes a good mix of general and special courses in your major field. When you want to expand into another area— taking an art class, for example— you may wish to use the pass-fail option for the course. This allows you to get a glimpse of that field with little risk.

4. Consider this analogy: Your education can be viewed as a part of a pyramid. The top of the pyramid represents what you want

to ultimately do with your life. A good, solid pyramid is built with a wide base. The safest way to the top is to get the base first and build on that.

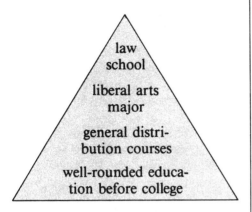

If anything goes wrong at the top—you can't get into law school, for example—you can back down a step and pursue another tack—teaching, or business administration.

A more daring approach to your career is to build a tall, skinny pyramid to the top. This is what Type A's do.

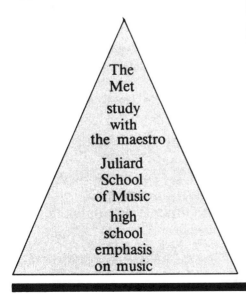

If the maestro dies before you get to him or Beverly Sills decides to rejoin the Met, your options are extremely limited after investing so much in your musical training.

This is not the wrong way to go. On the contrary, it is often the only way to go for the person with the right kind of drive and talent. Everyone, in light of his goals, will have to decide for himself. However, if you are a Type C who is pretty sure, but not totally closed to other options and opportunities, build your pyramid with a broad base and consider it insurance against a change of heart.

5. Continue to reevaluate your decisions as they are made.

I Walk the Line

College is a time to explore new opportunities. At the same time it is a place where decisions must be made, courses set and maturity gained.

You must find your own balance between personal goals and parental expectations; technical training and liberal education; current interests and occupational opportunities; preparation for employment and preparation for life.

Here we have just begun to address the issue. As a next step we recommend that you consider the following books which will be helpful as you seriously contemplate your future after leaving school. They offer additional information and practical exercises to help in career and life planning.

PRACTICAL CAREER PLANNING RESOURCES

Whether you need to assess your skills and interests, construct a résumé, scan job postings, or prepare for an interview, the resources are out there in abundance. Check out your campus career and placement center library and public library. Don't miss the on-line smorgasbord of frequently updated information and suggested resources. Here are a few ideas to get you started.

BOOKS
What Color Is Your Parachute? A Practical Manual for Job Hunters and Career Changers by Richard N. Bolles, Ten Speed Press (updated annually).

This best seller has been helping folks for over twenty-five years with job-hunting, interview prep, other practical helps, and warm encouragement.

Do What You Are: Discover the Perfect Career for You Through the Secrets of Your Personality Type by Paul D. Tieger and Barbara Barron-Tieger, second edition, Little, Brown & Co. (1995).

Learn more about yourself and the principle that certain jobs require certain personalities.

The Princeton Review's Student Access Guides—

Top titles include *America's Top 100 Internships, The Internship Bible, Don't Be a Chump: Negotiating Skills You Need, Trashproof Résumés,* and *How to Survive without Your Parents' Money.*

Knock 'Em Dead by M. J. Yate, Exec-U-Net (1993).

Excellent advice on how to prepare for an interview.

SOFTWARE

Kaplan Career Counselor, Kaplan Educational Centers

Comprehensive help on matching your skills to job descriptions.

WinWay Résumé 4.0, WinWay Corporation

Complete help on writing and sending out résumés, plus job description sections.

PFS: Résumé Pro Version 2, Softkey International

Includes four modules: Résumé Builder, Résumé Counselor, Job Search Manager, and Career Counselor.

OCCUPATIONAL OUTLOOK HANDBOOK

The United States Deparment of Labor yearly compiles vital information about the state of the nation (job-wise), and the Occupational Outlook Handbook is the resulting document.

It's huge, it's amazing, it's helpful! A concise analysis of hundreds of occupations, from nature of the work to working conditions; training needed to earnings expected; present state of employment to outlook for the future; related occupations to sources of additional information.

There's no better place to discover where insurance salespeople are thriving, where RNs are languishing or where welders are in greatest demand.

This publication is updated annually for the obvious reasons. Make sure you're working from this year's edition!

FIFTY QUESTIONS

Well, it's a little like twenty questions. It's a game you have to play with the folks who have a job opening that you would like to fill. Frank S. Endicott, retired director of Northwestern University's Placement Center, has developed a listing of the questions most commonly asked in job interviews with college seniors. How many can you answer? Be prepared!

1. What are your long-range and short-range goals and objectives, when and why did you establish these goals, and how are you preparing yourself to achieve them?

2. What specific goals, other than those related to your occupation, have you established for yourself for the next ten years?

3. What do you see yourself doing five years from now?

4. What do you really want to do in life?

5. What are your long-range career objectives?

6. How do you plan to achieve your career goals?

7. What are the most important rewards you expect in your business career?

8. What do you expect to be earning in five years?

9. Why did you choose the career for which you are preparing?

10. Which is more important to you, the money or the type of job?

11. What do you consider to be your greatest strengths and weaknesses?

12. How would you describe yourself?

13. How do you think a friend or professor who knows you well would describe you?

14. What motivates you to put forth your greatest effort?

15. How has your college experience prepared you for a business career?

16. Why should I hire you?

17. What qualifications do you have that make you think that you will be successful in business?

18. How do you determine or evaluate success?

19. What do you think it takes to be successful in a company like ours?

20. In what ways do you think you can make a contribution to

our company?

21. What qualities should a successful manager possess?

22. Describe the relationship that should exist between a supervisor and those reporting to him or her.

23. What two or three accomplishments have given you the most satisfaction? Why?

24. Describe your most rewarding college experience.

25. If you were hiring a graduate for this position, what qualities would you look for?

26. Why did you select your college or university?

27. What led you to choose your field of major study?

28. What college subjects did you like best? Why?

29. What college subjects did you like least? Why?

30. If you could do so, how would you plan your academic study differently? Why?

31. What changes would you make in your college or university? Why?

32. Do you have plans for continued study? An advanced degree?

33. Do you think that your grades are a good indication of your academic achievement?

34. What have you learned from participation in extracurricular activities?

35. In what kind of work environment are you most comfortable?

36. How do you work under pressure?

37. In what part-time or summer jobs have you been most interested? Why?

38. How would you describe the ideal job for you following graduation?

39. Why did you decide to seek a position with this company?

40. What do you know about our company?

41. What two or three things are most important to you in your job?

42. Are you seeking employment in a company of a certain size? Why?

43. What criteria are you using to evaluate the company for which you hope to work?

44. Do you have a geographical preference? Why?

45. Will you relocate? Does relocation bother you?

46. Are you willing to travel?

47. Are you willing to spend at least six months as a trainee?

48. Why do you think you might like to live in the community in which our company is located?

49. What major problem have you encountered, and how did you deal with it?

50. What have you learned from your mistakes?